D0120131

Guide to the
I Ching

BROCKHAMPTON PRESS
LONDON

© 1997 Geddes & Grosset Ltd,
David Dale House, New Lanark, Scotland

This edition published 1997 by Brockhampton Press, a member of
the Hodder Headline PLC Group

ISBN 1 86019 721 3

Printed and bound in India

Contents

Introduction

In today's cynical global business world it may come as a surprise to learn that some young executives on Hong-Kong's hi-tech stock-exchange regularly consult the ancient Chinese text of the I Ching (pronounced 'ee ching') for advice and guidance in their business and personal lives. A further surprise may be that they use the latest in state-of-the-art, hand-held computer technology with an electronic-text version of the I Ching! This might be dismissed as a harmless or frivolous use of modern technology, similar to electronic games. But those who regularly consult their electronic versions of the I Ching do so in a spirit of serious and thoughtful quest. For them it is no game. They bring specific questions to the I Ching, consulting it to find answers relevant to their situation and circumstances. Millions of others across the world consult their traditional text versions of I Ching to do likewise. Is this mere superstition, akin to the reading of newspaper and magazine horoscopes? Or is there more to it?

All of us at times in our lives find ourselves in situations where we feel the need of advice and guidance about what decisions to make, and what actions to take. Often we turn to others, whether it be friends, relatives, trusted colleagues or professional counsellors. But sometimes we hanker after some more profound guidance; something that would be impossible or inappropriate to ask or expect from anyone who knows us, yet neither would it be useful to consult a counsellor as some intimate knowledge of our inner selves is a prerequisite for the guidance we seek. In situations like these you will tend to rely on the person who knows you best: yourself. Some will augment this self-counselling with the spiritual dimension of prayer. Others will remain reliant on their own counsel and decisions, inadequate as they may prove to be. The I Ching provides another resource for advice and guidance, for help in deciding what to do in any particular situation, which many—in the West as well as the East—also use to help orient themselves towards their true directions and their true selves.

There is a spiritual dimension to the I Ching as well as a practical aspect to it, but using the I Ching has nothing to do with invoking the supernatural or calling on the help of benign spirits. What it is about, though, is consulting and trusting a system that was developed over many centuries and which displays remarkable and profound insights into the motives, attitudes and behaviour of individual and groups of people. For those who regularly consult it, the I Ching is valuable because they believe it to be practical and useful. For its millions of users there is nothing otherworldly about the I Ching; for them the I Ching quite simply works—and that is something that cannot be objectively defined or dismissed.

This book is intended as an introduction to familiarize you with the basic precepts and method of the I Ching. Like the I Ching itself, this book does not set out to provide you with definitive answers, either to your personal questions or to sceptical questions you may have about the I Ching. Its intention is not to provide irrefutable proof that the I Ching 'works'. It is hoped, though, that this book will help you to make up your own mind, not only about the answers you receive to your personal questions, but about the whole philosophy and method of the I Ching.

The creative use of chance events is the starting point in the method of consulting the I Ching. The consulter composes a question of some importance to her or his life. Then a series of chance events are enacted, in the form of the random disposals of cast yarrow stalks or thrown coins. The I Ching then sets out to interpret the meanings for the individual who initiates these chance occurrences. The I Ching becomes the guide or oracle which helps the individual to interpret these meanings.

The first step in this is to translate the results of the casting of coins, or the more traditional yarrow stalks, into patterns of broken and unbroken lines of the same length. If casting coins, heads will be assigned a solid line and tails a broken line. The outcome is two six-line figures called hexagrams. There is a system of sixty-four possible hexagrams. (Each hexagram is composed of two three-line figures called trigrams. There is a system of eight possible trigrams.) The first of the two hexagrams will offer an answer to your question as it affects your present situation; the second hexagram offers advice pertaining to future conditions. The I

Ching provides a system of analysis and commentaries for every hexagram. This system is consulted for the interpretation of each particular hexagram that is drawn from the casting of the coins or stalks. The consulter must then consider how the interpretation of the particular hexagram relates to the specific question she or he brought to the consultation. This is important. The I Ching does not provide cast-iron answers, give injunctions or make firm predictions: its role is to provide guidance and advice which will help an individual come to her or his own judgements or decisions concerning the question they have posed for themselves.

Nature of I Ching

The I Ching translates literally into English as *The Book of Changes*. Its theme is change—paradoxically the only constant and dependable thing in life—and regeneration, i.e., how one should respond to or deal with the changes one will inevitably face in life. This is the purpose of the I Ching: to help those who consult it learn from and benefit from change and to develop positive responses to change, no matter whether the change itself is considered negative or positive. This can be done by learning how to go with change (to 'go with the flow') rather than directly opposing it or resisting it; to learn how to turn change, to manipulate it, to one's advantage. To deal with change in this way is to be truly creative, both in the present and for the future. You are able to let go or free yourself from the past, from ways of thinking, feeling and behaving that are no longer relevant or rewarding, but are stagnant, stultifying and even harmful. The I Ching offers to help an individual change things in the present and thus alter their future.

In the context of a specific consultation of the I Ching, one of three possible kinds of fundamental change that affect any situation is uncovered: either non-change, cyclical change or sequential change. A non-change situation does not mean that there is no forward movement in time, no change—that would be impossible, but that things change only within the existing framework or system of things, which itself is not subject to change for the time being. Cyclical change happens in the same way as seasonal change. And sequential change is progressive change, as when one generation is superseded by the next, younger generation, in the nature of cause and effect. The I Ching also focuses on the role and the meaning of significant coincidences in relation to change.

When someone wants advice or guidance on a matter of importance, before they make a crucial choice or decision, they consult the I Ching. The I Ching is used as a kind of oracle, providing wise and authoritative answers to questions, and divining the outcome of present situations or events. But with the I Ching the person who consults is like a partner in the oracular consultation, participating in the process and interpreting and assessing the results for themselves in the light of their own self-knowledge and intuition. The I Ching is not a substitute for self-knowledge, or the responsibilities of free-will and autonomous decision-making; it is, rather, a valuable ally in this often difficult and lonely process.

The I Ching does not specifically predict or prescribe what the future outcome of any present situation will be. Rather, it indicates what it believes are suitable courses of action to take in any particular situation, and in so doing invites us to consider its suggestions, giving them careful thought before we come to our final decision about which course to take and which choice to make.

The text of the I Ching would be more accurately termed a collection of texts, written and expanded through different periods of early and later Chinese history. The I Ching is the most ancient and venerable book in Chinese culture, written and added to over many centuries. It is a compendium of historically accumulated learning and understanding, a lore of wit and wisdom, composed of a rich mixture of poetry, philosophy, psychology, worldly wisdom, practical advice, social insight and understanding. Because of its importance to the Chinese philosophies of Confucianism and Taoism and its status as one of the Five Classics of Chinese literature, the I Ching was preserved in China down through the ages. With its earliest parts dating from five thousand years ago it is older than the Bible, and though it is not a religious text it has been as revered in China as the Bible has been in the West. But, unlike the books of the Bible, the I Ching is not meant to be read straight through. In modern-day parlance the I Ching could be called an 'interactive text': we do something with it beyond the usual activities involved in reading and studying a text.

The basis of the I Ching

The fundamental basis of the I Ching, its underlying philosophy, is the belief that chance events are in fact not that: they are not random or accidental, meaningless or trivial occurrences, but are, in fact, significant and meaningful. It is held that all seemingly random occurrences are actually fundamentally and meaningfully connected to everything else that occurs at the same moment of time as they do; that is, simultaneous events have a connection above and beyond the basic fact that they are contemporaneous, and this connection has nothing to do with notions of cause and effect. Therefore, says the I Ching, it is possible to gain insight into the underlying forces that are influencing change in our lives by properly interpreting the significance and meaning of apparently chance events in our lives. These enable a link or an influence to be divined or perceived between the state of our subjective psychic and spiritual lives and the principles of change that are affecting us. This is where the I Ching comes in. Its role is to interpret properly the significance of chance events in your life. These are the key to identifying the relation between the events and circumstances of your life at the moment and the corresponding underlying forces of change. Randomness is the route to insight, significance and meaningful order.

To a sceptical frame of mind brought up in the dominant Western tradition of rationalism this may all seem a bit far-fetched and nonsensical, to say the least. Yet the concept of 'synchronicity' was treated seriously by the famous psychoanalyst and scholar, Carl Gustav Jung, who was enthusiastic about the I Ching. Like the I Ching, his theory of synchronicity stressed the connectedness of seemingly disparate or chance events with every other event they were simultaneous with, and insisted that this simultaneous link was significant and meaningful and not just a matter of coincidence. For the theory of synchronicity, there is no such thing as 'mere' coincidence. If anyone thinks about it they can recognize moments of such 'synchronicity' in their own lives. These are often, in fact, dismissed as moments of mere coincidence, though occasionally people have more startling encounters with what appears as uncanny coincidences. We can all provide examples of routine coincidences from our own or others experiences. For example, thinking about someone and then receiving a letter or telephone call from them, or actually bumping into them; or seeking the answer to some question and suddenly finding it turning up unprompted and unlooked for in some unexpected source. For Jung, then, there was nothing 'mere' about such coincidental incidents and happenings. For him (and for the I Ching) they are expressions of a kind of order that goes beyond the logical world of cause and effect. Synchronicity states that simultaneous events are linked not just by the fact that they occur at the same time but in terms of their mutual influence and their integration into a comprehensive meaning that is greater than its parts. It follows then that it is possible that answers to problems can be found not by looking at questions of cause and effect, but by observing and noting, and judging the significance of everything present at the same moment of time—sidestepping conventional logic entirely. (Traditional riddles, and imagery, poetry and metaphor similarly 'sidestep' the more limited, prosaic world of logical reality.) So that events that may seem unconnected, trivial or peripheral to the essential or central concerns and agendas of our lives at any given moment, are in fact significantly related synchronically to whatever we are thinking, feeling and doing at that particular moment, and all of these elements are ordered in relation to each other by the higher or fundamental creative forces which govern all change and thus all life.

Problem-solving

Modern theories of creative thinking and problem-solving, such as lateral thinking, employ methods similar to the I Ching's use of random occurrence as a route into insight and understanding: they seek ways of side-stepping the walls built up by commonsense and rationalism eg. the injunction to 'think outside the lines', if one is vainly struggling to solve a particularly difficult problem.

A little imaginary scenario might serve to illustrate here. Let's say, as a test of someone's problem-solving ability, he is faced with a cunningly devised, intricate knot tied in a piece of rope. Perplexed but determined, he is persevering with what seems the obvious method of tackling this literally knotty problem, i.e., he is using the powers of his eyesight and his mind to guide his

thumbs, index fingers and fingernails to tug and unpick the stubborn knot—but with all his determination he is getting nowhere.
Then the magician steps forward, takes the ends of the rope and
with one sharp jerk: 'Hey presto!' the knot disappears. The volunteer may have thought that what he was doing was unpicking a
knot, but in reality he was only tying himself in knots. One could
call what the magician did mere 'trickery' but that it was a trick is
not the point of the example. Thinking in only one way, the un-
successful volunteer was unable to see what was actually there.
This example shows that that the solution to aproblem may not lie
in what seems to be the most straightforward approach. So exit
stage-left one embarrassed and remorseful volunteer.

A Gestalt psychologist, Karl Duncker coined the term 'functional fixedness' to describe a common source of difficulty in
problem-solving. If finding the solution requires that some object
or concept be used in a new and unfamiliar way, a 'fixation' or
closed mindset on the common and familiar usage may prevent
the new one from being seen.

Circumventing these closed mindsets is the preferred method
of creative problem-solvers. The mathematician Gyorgy Polya
introduced the idea that there are general techniques for solving
problems, which he called heuristics: procedures that often help
though they cannot guarantee success. (The dictionary describes
heuristic method as 'using or obtained by exploration of possibilities rather than by the application of set rules'; i.e. one discovers or makes up the rules as one goes along and only when you
reach your solution can you look back and identify the'rules'.)
One useful heuristic is working backward from the solution. If
the answer were known, what characteristics would it have to
have? Another important heuristic is to establish subgoals. Think
of some situation from which the solution might be easier to obtain, and work toward that situation first. Again, the whole
method of I Ching could be interpreted or described as an heuristic method of creative problem-solving.

In Gestalt theories of perception, problem-solving and creative
thinking the emphasis is not on step-by-step deduction, but on
close and non-analytical, synthesizing observations of particu-
lars, which are integrated into a whole that gives coherence and

meaning to the individual parts. And the whole has a meaning of its own which is, crucially, more than the sum of its constituent parts. Seemingly unconnected clues are integrated by a sudden moment of illuminating perception into a meaningful whole. For seeing and creating, therefore, the emphasis is not on analysis, but synthesis: integrating all the synchronous elements of a situation into a meaningful whole.

Also, Gestalt psychology emphasizes the creative, intelligent, and organizational aspects of problem solving and learning. Insight is interpreted as a sudden, solution to a problem through a creative combination of previously unrelated ideas. This description could be applied to the whole method of the I Ching, from the casting of the coins to the final pondering of the meaning of a hexagram.

Deliberately abjuring or abandoning the logical and analytical mindset is and has been a liberating experience for many creative artists and problem solvers. The logical gap is suddenly gone and meaning, insight and understanding are present and luminous. It is a method of artistic insight and creation that has great validity. One could study and analyse a problem and end up going in circles, whereas intuition leaps to the answer and the goal in an instant. Similarly I Ching employs the method of chance: arriving at the answer without seeming to have travelled.

For the logical mind this might seem too paradoxical and suspiciously simplistic. The scientific method requires objective and explicit demonstrations of how something is done; and if this cannot be provided then the method or procedure is not valid and cannot be believed or trusted. But there are areas of skill or connoisseurship in life where people demonstrably and successfully carry out tasks, but would be unable to explicitly explain to others the elements and method of how they do what they do: from learning how to balance on and ride a bike, to identifying wine by its vineyard and year. Their successful performance of the skill is their knowledge of it. Analysis is by comparison a meaningless irrelevance.

And so it is with the I Ching. If the I Ching works for you, then it works. How it works is of secondary or even, to some perhaps, no importance. All you need for it to work is a knowledge of the procedure and an open but reflective frame of mind.

History

How, when and where did the text and method of the I Ching originate? It all began with the trigrams, which are reputed to have been the life's work of the first Chinese Emperor Fu Hsi. He was also a teacher and scholar and his formulation of the trigrams is said to have been the culmination of life-long study dedicated to discovering the underlying principles of the universe. The inspiration of the lines that form the trigrams was supposedly the patterns in the shell of a tortoise.

The origin of the trigrams is described in the form of a 'creation-myth' involving the essential opposing energies or principles of yin and yang, which are the basis of all things, everything in the universe being generated from their polarity. Yin is feminine and has passive power; yang is masculine and has active power. Paradoxically, yin and yang are both opposing and complementary, as can be seen from the symbol which represents them.

Yin and yang are light and dark, night and day, masculine and feminine, positive and negative, and all other fundamental and creative polarities. In terms of cosmology yin is related to the moon and controls the earth, yang is related to the sun and controls the heavens.

The I Ching states that Great Primal Beginning created the two primary principles of yin and yang and two primary trigrams. These then generated four images which in turn generated the eight founding trigrams of the I Ching.

Fu Hsi's original trigrams were expanded in a later period of early Chinese history by a feudal lord called King Wen and his son, the Duke of Chou. Shortly before 1,000 years BC they developed the three-line trigrams into six-line figures and created a system of sixty-four hexagrams. Each hexagram was given a distinctive name and a commentary was provided for each one which explained it and gave advice. In the I Ching this is known as the T'uan or the Judgement. There is also a commentary on the Judgement and the individual lines of each hexagram, which is known as Hsiang

yin and yang

Chuan or the Image. It is believed that the text of the I Ching attributed to King Wen and his son includes material which in fact originates from multiple authors beginning centuries before their time. So the I Ching incorporates aspects of ancient Chinese culture, many thousands of years old, in the form of oracular systems, ancient historical writings and poems.

Some centuries later, about the beginning of the fifth century BC, a further series of commentaries were written about the text of King Wen and added to the I Ching. These are known the T'uan Chuan or the Ten Wings and are attributed to the legendary Chinese philosopher and sage, Confucius, who was a great student of the I Ching. His contribution to the I Ching led it to become even more popular in China as a system of oracular divination.

The I Ching survived a barbaric period in Chinese history which was catastrophic for other texts, when in 213 BC the Emperor Ch'in Shih Huang Ti of the Chin dynasty (221-206 BC) ordered a massive book-burning. Many ancient and important works of Chinese literature and culture were disastrously destroyed, including many copies of the I Ching. Fortunately, enough copies survived.

As one of the few texts of Chinese culture that were left after the barbaric book-burning (at this period, like other texts prior to the invention of paper, the I Ching would have been written on strips of wood or bamboo), the I Ching became the object of even more scholarly devotion. Further commentaries and text were added by the adherents of Taoist philosophy as well as those by Confucianists and other schools of thought during the civilized and creative Han dynasty (202 BC-220 AD) which followed the barbarous Chin period. By the end of the second century AD imperial edict had ensured that the I Ching and four other classic texts associated with Confucianism were engraved in stone so that their wisdom would never be lost to humankind.

During later periods in Chinese history further commentaries continued to be added to the I Ching, most notably by the philosopher Chu Hsi during the Sung dynasty (960-1279). It is reported that by the early eighteenth century the I Ching included commentaries by over two hundred different scholars, dating back to the second century BC.

The I Ching was first introduced to the West in the early eighteenth century in France but it wasn't until its discovery in China by a German Christian missionary called Richard Wilhelm, in the late nineteenth century, that it became more widely known. Wilhelm translated the I Ching into German in the early years of this century and this became the basis for subsequent editions in English. There was an independent English translation published in 1899 by the English scholar and sinologist, James Legge but, good as it was, the fact that it was directed at an audience of other academics rather than the more popular readership that the Wilhelm translation achieved, meant that it has had less influence and is less well-known than the Wilhelm version.

The English translation of Wilhelm's German version of the I Ching was published in the late nineteen forties. It gained a steadily growing group of readers. But there was an explosive increase in the readership of the English I Ching during the late nineteen-sixties to the early nineteen-seventies. This wider popular Western audience arose during the heyday of the 'counter-culture' in the late sixties and early seventies, when the I Ching was adopted by adherents of the 'counter-culture' as a cult text and activity. Rejecting traditional Western culture—its values, religions, politics and philosophies—the 'counter-culture' movement sought new, more relevant and meaningful routes to insight, personal growth and wisdom. The I Ching—coming from the tradition of Eastern, Oriental culture and philosophy—had an immediate appeal, reinforced by its aura of ancient and exotic wisdom and its implicit challenge to what was seen as the authoritarian and arid logic and rationalism, and empty materialism of Western society.

The name and fame of the I Ching spread and developed throughout the widely-dispersed, international communities of the West's 'counter-culture', at first mainly by word of mouth, but increasingly in print—in 'alternative' newspapers and magazines—where the I Ching was discussed and advocated as a meaningful and worthwhile activity. It was regarded as a valuable practice for those intent on changing their lives by instilling new orientations and values into their lives, those seeking something more positive and fulfilling than what was currently on offer in the Western world. The I Ching also became of interest for many in the wider community, those who were on the alert for whatever was culturally new and intriguing, or for whatever might be, or might become, fashionable. Even in mainstream newspapers and magazines I Ching was generally at the very least treated respectfully as something worth investigation and consideration.

Today, when many former hippies, counter-culturalists and alternative lifestylers have become mainstream businesswomen and businessmen, with several of them running major international companies and corporations (I am not, of course, suggesting that consulting the I Ching was their means of finding the royal road to success, riches and fame!), the I Ching has broadened its appeal and reputation from that of a narrow and defining cult text to one that has become more widely known and available. Now, though, the I Ching has also become associated with the philosophies and activities, and sometimes downright 'fads', that go together to make up what is known as New Age lifestyles and philosophies. This is not to denigrate the concerns and activities of those interested in New Age ways of thinking about the world and of living in the world. But it would be fair to say that only a minority of people could be described as advocates or adherents of New Age culture. Perhaps because of this, many people who have heard, somehow, of the I Ching are still unaware of what it really is. To many it may still appear as something exotic and remote, and they are therefore tempted or inclined to dismiss it as an esoteric, frivolous or just plain daft text or activity, unconnected with the realities of ordinary living and daily life. This, though, would be a mistake; these fallacious views are exactly the opposite of what the I Ching is about.

This introductory text will go some way perhaps to remedying any misconceptions about the nature and purpose of I Ching, challenging and dissolving any preconceived ideas and false and erroneous views by providing an interesting and useful introduction to what I Ching really is and what you can do with it.

The original translated versions of the I Ching were faithful renditions of the full I Ching and the same is true of most modern editions. This, though, causes difficulties for the contemporary novice reader of the I Ching, who invariably has problems following and understanding the text. The language, even in a good translation, can seem frustratingly enigmatic and arcane, with obscure passages of poetry and puzzling metaphor. The rhetoric or the style of the language used can also cause problems, as can the many baffling references in the text. Some of these difficulties arise from the original historic audience and purpose of the textual commentaries made by King Wen and others. These writings are concerned with managing change as rulers of ancient Chinese kingdoms, and the language they are couched in and the references they use, such as to the political situation of their times, reflect this. Many aspects of the text, then, can only be understood with a knowledge of their historical context. The order of the various sections of the unabridged I Ching can also present problems.

Consequently it is usual, and more sensible, for novice readers of the I Ching to begin with an introductory text that serves as a bridge to the full I Ching, a preliminary step to future unaided explorations of the original and unabridged text. An introductory book such as the present one allows the novice to get more quickly to the heart of the method and meaning of the I Ching.

The three chapters that follow will do the following: the first will describe and discuss the methods for beginning the consultation of the I Ching; this leads on to a consideration of the trigrams in chapter two; and this in turn leads on to a description and discussion of the hexagrams in chapter three, including a list of the sixty-four hexagrams and their textual commentaries.

Each of the chapters will have more to say about the history, methods and philosophy of the I Ching from their own particular angle and in more depth and breadth of reference than the introduction. It is hoped that this will lead to an accumulating understanding and appreciation of what the I Ching is about as you read through the book. This will also lead to some inevitable overlap between the chapters. However, it is felt that this kind of reiteration or reinforcing of certain facts and concepts has a positive value which outweighs the fact of their repetition.

One last point—if you do find any of the discussions of the philosophy and method of the I Ching heavy-going, then skip them and carry on with the basic consultation of the hexagrams. The discussions of method and philosophy are important and relevant, but you can always come back to these sections later and read and ponder them at your leisure.

Consulting the I Ching

The first thing that has to be done is to decide what you want to consult the I Ching about. Remember, it should not be a trivial or frivolous matter, but concern something of real importance for the course of your life. Having chosen a subject for the consultation, you then have to frame this correctly as a specific question that the I Ching will be able to answer. This is crucial. It is fruitless and pointless to approach the I Ching with questions seeking a yes/no answer or an answer that will absolve you or remove the onus from you of involvement in making your own decisions. Also, avoid vague or generalized questions along the lines of, 'What should I do about my job/relationship/life?' Instead, compose specific questions like: 'What will happen if I leave this job?'; or, 'How will marriage affect our relationship?'; or, 'What will be the outcome if I decide to live abroad?'. You should formulate your question so that it will have a specific answer rather than a number of possibilities. Take your time, if necessary, over the wording of your question. Write it down if it helps to make the process easier.

Having formulated your question to your satisfaction you are now ready to begin the consultation. There are two main ways of doing this: the more traditional but time-consuming method using fifty yarrow sticks, which takes between half an hour and an hour; or the quicker and easier way using three coins, which takes only a few minutes or so.

The comparative ease and relative quickness of the coin method makes it the method preferred by most people nowadays. This will be described first, and then a description of the yarrow sticks method will follow.

Coin method

The coins you use can be Chinese coins if you like, but it is not necessary. Any three coins will do. For the purposes of the throw, the 'heads' side of the coin is the yang side, and the 'tails' side of

the coin is the yin side. You take the three coins and shake them in
your hand, then throw them onto a flat surface whenever you feel
like doing so. You then note and record which side of the coins
are uppermost. There are four possible combinations in which the
coins can land:

1. heads	heads	heads
2. tails	tails	tails
3. heads	tails	tails
4. tails	heads	heads

Each of these possible combinations is assigned a yin or yang
line-value. Remember, yin is represented by a broken line and
yang by a solid line. At this point, reference must be made to what
are known as 'moving lines', and also to 'old' and 'young' lines.
But it would complicate matters too much at this initial stage in
learning the method of consulting the I Ching to take into account
'moving lines' etc. They will, though, be discussed later. For the
time being we will follow the procedure of drawing two hexagrams for each consultation: the first will present an answer to a
question as it applies to the circumstances of the present; the second will offer advice concerning future conditions.

The line values which are assigned to each of the four possible heads and tails combinations depend on whether it is the
hexagram of the present or the hexagram of the future. The following table gives the line values for the present and future
hexagrams.

Coin Combination	Present Hexagram	Future Hexagram
1. heads heads heads	solid line (yang)	broken line (yin)
2. tails tails tails	broken line (yin)	solid line (yang)
3. heads tails tails	solid line (yang)	solid line (yang)
4. tails heads heads	broken line (yin)	broken line (yin)

In order to construct your two hexagrams—the first for the
present, the second for the future—you must throw the coins six
times and record the result of each throw as yin or yang line values for the present hexagram and for the future hexagram. The
following example shows what this might look like, depending
on the outcome of your throws.

Coin Combination	Present Hexagram	Future Hexagram
1. tails heads heads	yin (bottom line)	yin (bottom line)
2. heads tails tails	yang (second line)	yang (second line)
3. tails heads heads	yin (third line)	yin (third line)
4. heads heads heads	yang (fourth line)	yin (fourth line)
5. heads tails tails	yang (fifth line)	yang (fifth line)
6. heads tails tails	yang (top line)	yang (top line)

You begin building each six-line hexagram from the bottom line up, beginning with the line values for your first throw, the second line will be from the line values of your second throw, and so on as shown in the table above. The following two hexagrams are built from the results of the throws recorded above.

Present Hexagram

Future Hexagram

Generating hexagrams in this way is relatively quick and uncomplicated. It is the preferred method if you are interested in getting the hexagrams built as quickly as possible so that you can look up the judgements and interpretations and relate these to the question you have posed. There are other reasons, though, why some prefer using the casting of yarrow sticks to build the hexagrams. The description of the yarrow stick procedure which follows also includes an analysis of its appeal to those who use it.

Yarrow Stick Method

The yarrow sticks method uses a bundle of fifty sticks of the same length. Stalks from the yarrow plant (Achillea millefolium) were used because, according to legend, the yarrow plant grew on the grave of Confucius. Traditionally, though, the sticks used were of bamboo or any suitable wood.

The correct traditional method of beginning to consult the I Ching using yarrow sticks is to face south and place the text of the I Ching in front of you, with the yarrow sticks and a burning incense-candle by your right side. Take the yarrow sticks in your right hand and, keeping them horizontal, pass them through the smoke of the burning incense in a circular, clockwise movement. This is held to help with the formulation of the question. Place the sticks down and remove one stick from the bundle with your right hand and put it aside. This stick will not be used in the procedure, the remaining forty-nine sticks only being used.

You divide them randomly into two piles and place them right and left. Take a stick from the right-hand pile and place it between the little finger and the ring finger of the left hand. Then the left-hand pile is placeD in your left hand, and with your right hand you take from it bundles of four sticks at a time and lay them aside. You will end with a final group of four sticks or less. These should now be placed between the ring finger and the middle finger of the left hand. You then count through the right-hand pile in groups of four, laying them aside, and place the final group of four or less between the middle and index finger of the left hand. You will now have a total of either five or nine sticks held in the fingers of your left hand. (The various possible combinations are: 1+4+4, or 1+3+1, or 1+2+2, or 1+1+3. It can be seen, therefore, that the number 5 is more likely to be obtained than the number 9). Lay these sticks to one side for the time being.

Put all the remaining sticks back together in one pile and then divide randomly again into two piles. Then repeat the above process, beginning again by taking a stick from the right-hand pile and placing it between the ring finger and the little finger of the left hand. When you have finished, lay aside the pile of sticks you have placed in your left hand—you will have either four or eight sticks in total.(The possible combinations this time are: 1+4+3, or 1+3+4, or 1+1+2, or 1+2+1. It can be seen that there is a fifty-fifty chance of producing totals of either four or eight).

Then begin the whole process for a third time with the sticks that are remaining. The number of sticks in your left hand when you finish will again be either four or eight.

You will now have three small piles of sticks. Count the number of sticks in each pile. A pile of four or five sticks is assigned a value of 3. A pile of eight or nine sticks is assigned a value of 2. You then total the combined values of your three piles. You will finish with one of four possible numbers, from four possible combinations, in the following way:

Values	Total Value
2+2+2 =	6
3+3+2 =	8
2+2+3 =	7

The possible total values correspond to either yin or yang lines in the Present and Future hexagrams in the following way

Total Values	Present Hexagram	Future Hexagram
9	yang line	yin line
6	yin line	yang line
8	yin line	yin line
7	yang line	yang line

So, at this stage in your casting of the yarrow sticks you have derived a single number value from your counting of the numbers of sticks and this has been translated into yin or yang line values for the bottom line of your present and future hexagrams. To get the remaining five lines for each of your hexagrams you now have to repeat the whole procedure five times.

Certain questions are provoked by the yarrow stalks procedure of consulting the I Ching. The first obvious one is: 'If only forty-nine sticks are going to be used, then why begin with fifty?' A valid question. It would, indeed, seem illogical and absurd not to begin with forty-nine sticks in the first place, if that is the number of sticks which are going to be used. Logic has nothing to do with this initial procedure or with the whole procedure of I Ching, whose stress on the value and meaning of chance occurrence is a challenge to the intellectual and cultural system which affirms the all-explanatory value of logic and rational common-sense. I Ching proceeds deliberately by the illogical. In the realms of the non-logical, the symbolic and the metaphorical other kinds of meaning, other kinds of perception of reality are possible which are not open to the exclusively logical and rational.

The simple removal of one stick from the fifty is held to gener-ate symbolic significance and meaning, as well as mystical power. Firstly, the forty-nine sticks left have a mystical signifi-cance and power, as forty-nine is the number seven squared and seven, in many traditional and ancient systems of belief and oracular divination, is regarded as a highly significant number in

terms of its mystical power. (The mystical significance of numbers will not be dealt with especially in this text. There are,
though, many texts on the subject of numerology if you are interested in finding out more.) Secondly, there is a symbolic aspect to
beginning with fifty and then taking one away, that emulates the
complementary polarities of yin and yang, the energies or principles
which generate all meaning, all things. Beginning with the whole
and then making it less than whole, creates a difference, a change
between what was whole and what is now not whole. Difference
is the moment of the birth of perception, hence of possibility and
the future of creation. All change is the outcome of difference, deriving from that essential difference between yin and yang, and
change is the source of all meaning, all life. Thus removing the
stick is a highly auspicious thing to do, symbolically emulating
the all-generating, mutually influencing opposition of yin and yang.

The yarrow sticks method is a more time-consuming and complicated method of beginning the consultation but it has its attractions and its adherents. The routine of repeated actions creates a
ceremonial sense which some find appealing. There is also the
satisfaction some derive from the feeling of following in a long
and hallowed tradition when using the yarrow sticks. And some
prefer the yarrow sticks method for the opportunity it allows for
meditation and reflection during the period it takes to build the
hexagrams. To many, though, it is simply the sense of symbolic
and mystical power that the yarrow stick method generates that
makes it the preferred method.

There are other traditional methods of consulting the I Ching
which have been used by the Chinese; for example, using grains
of rice or using marked 'wands'. The latter has some similarities
with the yarrow stick method as the wands are sticks of the same
length, but only six are used and they are painted black with a
white bar across one side. (If you think of stage magicians' wands
then you have made an interesting connection with something
similar; the magician's wand, though, is a black rod with a long
white tip.) The bundle of wands is thrown onto the ground. Then,
beginning with the nearest, they are picked up in turn. If the white
bar is uppermost then that signifies a yin line otherwise they signify a yang line. And the order in which they are picked up is the

order of the lines in the hexagram, beginning as always with the bottom line. One disadvantage with this method is that it does not incorporate a means of providing lines for two hexagrams—for the present and the future.

Whichever of the two main methods described you decide to use, the outcome will be that you have drawn two six-line hexagrams, building them up from the bottom line. This way of constructing the hexagrams probably derives from the Chinese system of writing characters, but it is likely it is also intended to symbolize or emulate the direction of most natural growth: from the earth to the sun.

Some practice in the method of drawing a hexagram would be appropriate at this point before we move on. Initially, we will use the coin method, and concentrate on drawing a present hexagram only. We will assume that you have thrown the coins and have obtained the following results:

first throw—two heads and one tail
second throw—two heads and one tail
third throw—one heads and two tails
fourth throw—three tails
fifth throw—two heads and one tail
sixth throw—three heads.

Now we will look at the hexagram these values translate into, starting from the bottom line, which is your first throw, and working our way up, as follows:

Hexagram 52
Ken—The mountain

The sixth throw gives a solid yang line.
The fifth throw gives a broken yin line.
The fourth throw gives a broken yin line.
The third throw gives a solid yang line.
The second gives you broken yin line.
The first throw gives you a broken yin line.

The methods described so far will enable you to begin immediately consulting the individual hexagrams in the hexagram system, reading the commentaries and pondering the meanings in relation to the questions you pose. However, it is now time to bring in the significance of what was referred to in passing earlier—'moving lines'. Their role in creating a 'future' hexagram as well as one for the present has to be explored and explained.

(You may wish to read and digest this information before you first build a hexagram—in which case you will use the method that relates to this—or you may prefer to begin with one of the methods already outlined above and come back to this section of the text later. The choice is yours).

Moving Lines Method

The aspect of the hexagram lines we will be looking at here is whether they are what is known as 'moving lines'. For individual lines this means they are referred to in one of four possible ways: 'old yang' and 'old yin'; or 'young yang' and 'young yin'. The moving lines are the lines that are not fixed. So, young yin and young yang are the lines in their unchanging form, confirmed in their polar positions of yin and yang, respectively. But old yin and old yang are in the process of changing into their polar opposite. When the yin or yang power attains its zenith, it becomes 'old'. At which point it changes to its polar opposite.

An old yin line in a hexagram is shown as an unbroken line with an 'x' in the centre, as follows: ▬▬▬✕▬▬▬

And an old yang line is drawn as an unbroken line with a small circle in the centre, as follows: ▬▬▬Ο▬▬▬

So an old yin line is in the process of moving from yin to yang and will become a yang line; and similarly, an old yang line is in the process of moving from yang to yin and will become a yin line.

Earlier, in the descriptions of the coin and yarrow stick methods, we looked at how to translate the throws of the coins or yarrow sticks into yin or yang values in order to draw the lines of the hexagram. The translation method used was different in the yarrow sticks method as it assigned numeric values to heads and tails. This is also the method used if one wishes to build hexagrams which explicitly incorporate moving lines; and it can be used with coins as well as yarrow sticks.

When using the three coins, one throws them as before and notes how they fall in their particular combinations of heads and tails, with the heads side still being the yang side, and the tails side still being the yin side. This time though, the yang (heads) side is assigned the numeric value of 3; and the yin (tails) side is assigned the numeric value of 2. You count the value of each coin on this numeric basis, and then you add these values together. Thus each throw of the three coins will yield one of four possible values: six, seven, eight or nine. The hexagram lines for each value are drawn as below:

The top line is old yang and has a value of 9.
The broken line below is young yin and has a value of 8.
The solid line in second position is young yang and has a value of 7.
The bottom line is old yin and has a value of 6.

It is possible when you cast your coins, or yarrow sticks, to have no moving lines, because you have values of 8 or 7 for every throw and so you have a hexagram composed only of young yin and young yang lines. If so you would only draw one hexagram as this one refers to a situation that is static or ending.

It is more than likely, though, that when you cast the coins you will indeed get a moving line, which is a 6 or 9. 6 is old yin and the 9 is old yang. In this case you would draw the hexagram incorporating the moving lines. You would then draw a second hexagram, the same as the first except for the moving lines, which are changed into their 'young' opposites, i.e.: old yang becomes a broken yin line, and old yin becomes a solid yang line.

Six throws of the coins have obtained the following hexagrams:
first throw—two 3s and a 2 = line value of 8
second throw—three 2s = line value of 6 (moving line)
third throw—three 3s = line value of 9 (moving line)
fourth throw—two 2s and a 3 = line value of 7
fifth throw—two 3s and a 2 = line value of 8
sixth throw—two 2s and a 3 = line value of 7

2nd hexagram, with moving lines changed into 'opposite' values: the 2nd line is young yang, and the 3rd line is young yin.

1st hexagram, incorporating moving lines: 2nd line is old yin (6), and 3rd line (9) is old yang.

(As you will see later, the moving lines hexagram is known as the Ting hexagram; whereas the second hexagram is known as the Wei Chi hexagram).

You then have to read both hexagrams, by looking them up in the hexagram system. You will also have to read the meanings of the moving lines, but for the first hexagram only. You only need to take the line readings into account when you have moving lines in a hexagram. You will look at the reading for the line number where you have a moving line. The moving lines highlight areas of change and aspects of significant note. The moving lines indicate that the whole situation is unbalanced, being either too positive or too negative, and so is open to change. The second hexagram represents the change that will occur in the future.

Regarding the second or 'future' hexagram, it is appropriate here to take note of what James Legge said on this matter in the introduction to his translation of the I Ching: "The object of the divination ... was not to discover future events absolutely , as if they could be known beforehand, but to ascertain whether certain schemes, and conditions of events contemplated by the consulter, would turn out luckily or unluckily."

The intention of the I Ching was never to give authoritative predictions about what was going to occur in the future, but to indicate whether plans and actions initiated in the present were likely to turn out favourably. This is more in the nature of what is called a prognosis, meaning a plausible and valid assessment of the probability of a present situation having one future outcome as opposed to another.

Whatever method you use to generate hexagrams it is important to realize and remember that each hexagram is composed of an upper and lower trigram. The trigrams were the origin of the I Ching and each of the eight possible trigrams has a name and commentary assigned to it. Also, each possible individual line in a trigram has a name and associated commentary. In the next section we will take a closer look at the trigrams and their meanings, before moving on to consideration of the hexagrams themselves.

The Trigrams

The origins of the trigrams were single yin and yang lines which were used as oracles. In ancient times, oracles were a common feature of all cultures. (For example, in ancient Greece, there was famously the oracle of Apollo at Delphi). The oldest oracles committed themselves to simple yes or no answers to the questions they were posed. This type of oracular declaration was the origin of the lines of the trigram (and hence of the hexagrams and the I Ching).'Yes' was indicated by an unbroken (yang) line: ▬▬▬▬▬; and 'no' was a broken (yin) line: ▬▬ ▬▬. At some point though, it was felt necessary to have a greater degree of differentiation, and so the single lines were combined in pairs, which resulted in four possibilities:

▬▬ ▬▬   ▬▬▬▬▬   ▬▬ ▬▬   ▬▬▬▬▬

Later, a third line was added to these four combinations, thus producing the system of eight trigrams. (A list of the eight trigrams follows below). These trigrams were thought of as symbols or images that comprised everything that happens in heaven and earth. They were also regarded as being in a state of continual transition, one trigram changing into another. This embodies the continual transitions of one thing or state to another that are always happening in the real world.

This is the fundamental basis of the I Ching. The eight trigrams are symbols that represent transitional states. They are images that are always in the process of changing into another image. So in terms of how they relate to phenomena in the real world, the focus is not on things as they are, on their fixed nature; the concentration is not on an analysis of what the constituent parts are of any phenomenon, what causes and effects brought it into existence: this being the typical emphasis and concern of Western ways of thinking. In the trigrams and the I Ching the attention is instead on the movement of things in change. So the eight trigrams do not represent things in themselves, but the tendencies of these things in movement.

Each of the trigrams is assigned a specific name which corresponds to different processes in the natural world, such as fire, wind, thunder etc. A list of the eight possible trigrams, generated from all the possible combination of yin and yang lines, are given below, with their Chinese names in bold and their English translations in brackets.

Ch'ien (Heaven/ Sky)	K'un (Earth)	Chen (Thunder)	K'an (Water)

Ken (Mountain)	Sun (Wind)	Tui (Marsh/ Lake)	Li (Fire)

These are further classified into what are known as major and minor trigrams, according to their combination of strong yang lines and yielding yin lines. Their English names are as follows:

> Major yang trigrams: Heaven and Marsh
> Minor yin trigrams: Thunder and Fire
> Major yin trigrams: Earth and Mountain
> Minor yang trigrams: Water and Wind.

Each of the trigrams has a main attribute. For example: Heaven is the Creative, which is strong (yang); and Earth is the Receptive, which is yielding (yin). Each trigram also has different meanings and associations corresponding to different classes of phenomena in the natural, animal and human worlds. For example, there are different trigrams for the different functions associated with the family roles of mother, father, three sons and three daughters. To clarify this by example: the sons represent the different stages of the principle of movement: start of movement; danger in movement; and culmination of movement, rest. The

daughters signify the different stages of devotedness: gently penetrating or spreading; clarity and adaptability; and tranquil joy.

The following table lists the eight trigrams, with their names
and all the main attributes and key associations for each trigram.

Name	Ch'ien	K'un	Chen	K'an	Ken	Sun	Li	Tui
Signifies	heaven	earth	thunder	water	mountain	wind	fire	marsh
Attribute	creative/ strong	receptive/ yielding	arousing/ moving	abyss/ danger	unmoving/ resting	gentle/ pene- trating	separate/ clarifying	happy/ joyful
Animal	horse	cow	dragon	pig	dog	cat	bird	sheep
Season	early winter	early autumn	spring	winter	early spring	early summer	summer	autumn
Polarity	yang	yin	yang	yang	yang	yin	yin	yin
Element	metal	soil	grass	wood	stone	air	fire	flesh
Direction	north west	south west	east	north	north east	south east	south	west
Family member	father	mother	first son	middle son	third son	first daughter	second daughter	third daughter
Colour	purple	black	orange	red	green	white	yellow	blue
Body part	head	solar plexus	foot	ear	hand	thighs	eye	mouth

Ch'ien signifies supreme creative inspiration. Its three unbroken lines represent strength, vitality and good fortune. It also signifies completeness, coldness, power and forcefulness.

K'un is the opposite of Ch'ien. It is feminine and passive. It relates to yielding and nurturing, kindness, devotion and loyalty.

Chen is to do with movement and speed. It relates to expansion
and growth, impulsiveness and experimenting.

K'an signifies danger. It relates to depth of thought and concentration.

Ken represents completeness and stillness. It has to do with
caution, thoroughness and inevitability.

Sun relates to fauna and growth, flexibility and separateness.

Li represents clarity, beauty and enlightenment. It also relates
to clinging and resolution.

Tui signifies delight and joy, sensual pleasure and magical achievement, growth and success.

These then are the primary trigrams which in combination make up the sixty-four hexagrams of the I Ching. As well as the upper and lower primary trigrams of a hexagram, the original authors also took into consideration what is called a hexagram's nuclear trigrams. These consist of the lower nuclear trigram, made up of the second, third and fourth lines of the hexagram; and the upper nuclear trigram, made up of the third, fourth and fifth lines. Both primary trigrams and nuclear trigrams are indicated in the hexagram below.

Upper primary trigram: Sun {lines 4,5,6}
Upper nuclear trigram: Ken {lines 3,4,5}
Lower nuclear trigram: Chen {lines 2,3,4}
Lower primary trigram: Tui {lines 1, 2,3}

Identifying, analysing and discussing a hexagram's primary and nuclear trigrams, as well as their individual lines if they are moving lines, is the key activity of the I Ching. It is important to keep in mind that the I Ching's system of sixty-four hexagrams is entirely composed of the core system of primary trigrams in all their possible combinations. And it is the combined associations of the two primary trigrams that makes up the particular properties of a hexagram. The table that follows provides a key to all the possible hexagrams, with the upper and lower primary trigrams that make up each hexagram.

The next chapter provides an analysis and commentary for each of the sixty-four hexagrams, as well as further, elucidating discussion on the origins and philosophy of the hexagrams. When you have drawn a hexagram you can locate it in the table by finding its upper and lower trigrams and hence the number of the hexagram. You then use this number to find the hexagram in the system of hexagrams in the next chapter.

Key to the Hexagrams

UPPER TRIGRAMS / LOWER TRIGRAMS	chi'en	k'un	chen	k'an	ken	sun	tui	li
chi'en	1	11	34	5	26	9	43	14
k'un	12	2	16	8	23	20	45	35
chen	25	24	51	3	27	42	17	21
k'an	6	7	40	29	4	59	47	64
ken	33	15	62	39	52	53	31	56
sun	44	46	32	48	18	57	28	50
tui	10	19	54	60	41	61	58	38
li	13	36	55	63	22	37	49	30

The Hexagrams

This chapter deals with the sixty-four hexagrams of the I Ching. They are listed in numerical order, and an extensive textual commentary and interpretation accompanies each drawn hexagram. The significance of the hexagrams lies in their representative or symbolic nature. Each of the hexagrams symbolizes a transitional state in human life, and the hexagram system as a whole is the symbolic representation of a series of situations in human life. The hexagrams consist of six lines, and all the sixty-four possible hexagrams are derived from the core system of eight three-line trigrams, which themselves are derived from combinations of the basic solid yang line and broken yin line. Within the hexagram it is the 'movements' of these individual yang and yin lines (i.e., the 'moving lines' that were discussed earlier) that change one hexagram into another, thus signifying the change of one situation into another. Of course, as we have seen above, when a hexagram has no moving lines it means that, for the time being, there is no movement within the situation that it represents: it is not in the process of changing into another situation, and thus another hexagram. In this case, when reading the textual commentaries, only the meaning of the hexagram as a whole has to be considered, and not the individual lines.

Each hexagram has a Chinese name, with an English translation. The analysis and discussion of each hexagram covers three main areas: the Judgement (the Tuan of King Wen); the Image and Line Readings (the Hsiang Chuan of King Wen's son, the Duke of Chou); and the Interpretation (based on the T'uan Chuan, or Ten Wings, which is mainly attributed to Confucius and his followers).

The Judgement identifies the overall theme and the meaning of the hexagram, including its auspicious or inauspicious nature. The Image concentrates on discussion of the hexagram's symbolic content and analysis of individual lines. (Keep in mind that the only individual lines that are of importance are the moving lines; these are the lines that you will go to the line analysis for. The other, non-moving, lines in a hexagram have a purely functional role in constructing the hexagram). The Interpretation is based on the explanatory comments on the Judgement and the Image, called the T'uan Chuan; but it is used here give an interpretative account of the Judgement and also the structure of the hexagram.

At the head, though, of each section of discussion on a hexagram, you will find the 'Commentary'. This is a paragraph which is intended to collate or bring together in a convenient and readily understood form the import and meaning of the hexagram. It incorporates elements from all the other discussions and interpretations of the hexagram.

The section which follows below carries on from earlier discussions on the historical development of the method and philosophy of the I Ching. The ideas and information presented here are intended to deepen your understanding and appreciation of the I Ching. But, as has been said before, it is not necessary to know this material in order to consult the I Ching. Accordingly, if you would prefer at this point to move straight on to consideration of the actual hexagrams then you can skip the following section, which you can come back to any point. However, before immersing yourself in the hexagrams and their texts it would be useful and relevant to read the section immediately prior to the hexagram system, which can be found under the heading of, Final Points on the Text.

Development of the I Ching

The I Ching, as has been stated before, is not like an oracle that attempts to give yes or no answers, with their inevitable 'hit or miss' nature, to questions about the future. Still less is the I Ching involved in making specific predictions about the future, as in the business of clairvoyant prediction, with its—claimed—spectacular successes or, more probably, its ignominious failures. There is also an aspect of the game or the entertainment in this kind of prediction, involving the element of suspense as one waits to see whether the prediction is to be applauded or ridiculed in the light of actual events.

The fortune-teller or soothsayer, whether it be a person or an impersonal system which is consulted, sets out to make specific predictions about your future which are presented as your supposedly inevitable fate. You are the passive recipient of this fate; no action by you is involved in the appearance of this fated event or set of circumstances. So, for example, if you are informed that a pleasing sum of money is coming your way, or a welcome stranger will cross your path, then all you are expected to do is wait: for the prediction to come true—or not. The prediction requires no action of yours to bring it about. It is supposed to happen independently of you as your destined 'fate.' Nothing you do or do not do will have any effect whatsoever on this kind of prediction or 'fate'. This kind of soothsaying, then, has no moral aspect, in that it does not provide for an individual taking an action or actions that will have an effect on their good or bad fortune in the future. The good or bad aspects of your fortune signify nothing more than the good luck or bad luck doled out to you by the inscrutable workings of fate.

The I Ching, on the other hand, is not a soothsaying oracle. It is not a fortune-teller. It does not present you with 'facts' about your future, that are supposed to be your inevitable fate for good or ill. It is not a game, either, nor an entertainment. The I Ching is a serious and responsible means for putting the individual who consults it in the position of having to consider what courses of action to take in a situation. In other words, the I Ching is a text and a procedure that has a moral significance.

When someone, having successfully divined an oracular pronouncement of their good or bad fortune, then went on to ask in addition the question, 'What can I do?', he was introducing a moral element to the process of oracular consultation that had not been there before. He was also challenging the notion of unchangeable and inevitable fate by implying that an individual's action could have an outcome that would have an effect on his 'fate'. He was no longer content, therefore, to submit to the absolute and impersonal power of fate—he wanted to have an influence on the way things turned out. Fate was no longer something simply to be accepted for good or ill. The individual felt he now had the right and the power to intervene in his own fate, and he was searching for the means of doing that, seeking to find the best way of influencing and shaping his fate. This could mean either doing something to ensure that a predicted good fortune did in fact happen (perhaps in dissatisfied or frustrated response to previous situations where the predicted good fortune had failed to materialize); or, what was more likely, seeking to prevent or avoid a predicted misfortune. In other words, the individual wanted to intervene in order to consolidate his predicted fate or to change it. But would the oracle be able to help the individual by answering this new question regarding what he should do?

Before that question was fully satisfied, however, another aspect of the situation intruded to complicate matters. There was a double edge to this new sword that the individual had taken to the binding cords of the web of fate. The individual wanted to intervene in his own fate. But the appropriation of this right, also became an unavoidable obligation. The inescapable hand of fate was replaced by the inescapable obligation of having to act—in some way or another. In any situation it was no longer a choice of deciding whether one should or needed to do something. Something, now, had to be done. Taking responsibility for some course of action in every situation was now unavoidable. You could not pick and choose among situations to decide which ones you would be responsible for and which you would simply allocate to fate. Once you had admitted the proposition that you could have an influence on your fate, then that applied to any and all situations in which you found yourself. So now, faced with a bewildering and burdensome plethora of choices to make and actions to take in many situations, the individual needed some form of help.

The I Ching was able to provide that help. Not only did it undertake to answer the original question of, 'What can I do?', it offered to answer it with a comprehensive and systematic textual commentary that would be adequate for all possible courses of action, and thus would help to relieve the burden of individual choice as to the right course of action in any situation. It would help to relieve, but not replace the necessity of individual choice. The decision of what action to take in a situation was ultimately the responsibility of the individual. The I Ching gave guidance, but it issued no commands.

A means of guidance

In the history of the I Ching, it was King Wen and his son, the Duke of Chou, who enabled the hexagrams to fulfil a more sophisticated function, and thereby introduced the moral dimension to the I Ching. Prior to this the collection of hexagrams basically had been used as yea or nay oracles or as a soothsaying book, to divine individual futures—each of which was totally unrelated to another's, being absolutely specific to one individual; and this divined future required no action to bring it about. In place of this, King Wen and his son endowed the hexagrams with a text that provided guidance and advice on courses of action for an individual to take in a situation. This need for guidance stems, as we have seen above, from the recognition that came after the decisive role of 'fate' was discarded in favour of an individual's intervention in the course of his life—the recognition that each situation demanded the appropriate action.

In any possible situation, then, there is a right and a wrong course of action. The right course is that which brings good fortune and the wrong course is that which brings misfortune. But there is also a moral aspect to this that goes beyond the egotistic dwelling on the good or bad fortune of the individual. And that moral aspect is other people. The question about what course of action to take in a situation had now broadened to take into consideration other people. The I Ching's textual commentary incorporated this fully moral dimension, with specific direction on the correct conduct to take in any situation. This emphasis on correct conduct involved more than just taking the course of action that would be favourable to oneself; it also consisted of taking into account the effect on others of one's actions.

With the advent of this textual commentary to accompany the hexagrams, the I Ching went beyond being a book of mere fortune-telling, and emerged in a different and higher dimension as an authoritative and revered book of wisdom.

The I Ching's counsels for the right and proper conduct were answering a more profound and complex question than, 'What can I do?', with its exclusive, self-interested motives; the I Ching was now setting out to answer the question, 'What ought I to do?', with its implied sense of individuals in relation to each other in a community, and the awareness of there being moral imperatives arising from this. Asking what one should do is a moral question in that it implies our awareness of ourselves in relation to, and with, others. Therefore the recognition that all our actions have a dual significance in terms of their mutual effect on ourselves and others, and that these mutual effects will reverberate in the form of other actions and their mutual effects, and so on, and so on: the never-ending moral dimension.

The I Ching, then, is a book of moral intervention. It aims to help individuals have some influence at least on shaping the nature of their fate; and it firmly embeds this opportunity and obligation within an overall moral code that takes in the responsibilities that individuals have for each other as well as for themselves. By developing a sense of morality through responsible thinking about situations and taking morally judged actions, the individual would develop a sense of moral authority in himself—a conscience or moral intuition—which would become the final arbiter or moral authority in making moral choices and decisions.

Timing
The crucial factor in using the I Ching to help one intervene successfully in one's fate, was timing. The earlier one intervened in a situation with the correct action, the more likely it was that you would be able to shape it to your wishes—wishes that would be in concordance with the morally correct motives and actions advocated by the I Ching. Identifying this germinal phase of a situation is the key; and this is the key function of the I Ching. If situations are in their early stages then they can be controlled. Taking the appropriate action at this time will enable one to decisively influence outcomes. But if a situation is allowed to develop to its full consequences before we try to intervene in it—then it is too late. By this time the situation has an overwhelming momentum of its own and the only moral choice left is how to accommodate oneself to it, how to accommodate it in one's life.

The power of the I Ching
The I Ching, with the combined power of the hexagrams and the accompanying text, now had the power and the ability to divine, and put one who consults it in touch with, the forces of movement

and change that influenced human life. The hexagrams and their lines, with their movements and changes, were able to represent the movements and changes of the underlying or creative powers of the universe. And the I Ching allowed an individual to have an influence on these controlling influences.

The casting of the yarrow stalks which enabled an individual to 'tap into' the fundamental governing forces of his life had a two-fold significance. Its use of chance was a route into the non-logical, unconscious aspects of himself, which were at a profound level in tune with, in concordance with, the life-forces of the universe. And the yarrow-stalk itself was, literally, a divining rod. As a humble form of plant life it was a direct link to, and was a physical manifestation of, the life-force; and as a sacred plant it had a link with the fundamental spiritual principles of life.

The use of coins is also a good means of tapping into the revelatory power of chance, as the opposite sides are directly symbolic of the basic polarities which are the basis of the universe: yin and yang. Also, in their actual use, as well as being physical objects, coins are also symbolic objects, and so provide or represent that link between the physical and the spiritual which is at the heart of the process of consulting the I Ching.

The philosophy of the I Ching

The moral dimension, then, became an integral and fundamental aspect of the I Ching. The I Ching also had the avowed ability to divine or perceive the fundamental movements and changes of the universe and reproduce them, in the form of the hexagrams and their text, for the moral and spiritual benefit of those who consulted it. Thus was the I Ching established as an authoritative and revered book of wisdom. It was perceived and used as such by philosophers such as Lao-Tse, the founder of the philosophy and religion of Taoism. His thought and teaching were imbued with the wisdom of the I Ching, and it inspired him to some of his profoundest aphorisms. The ancient Chinese philosopher Confucius was also influenced and inspired by the I Ching. His famous aphorisms and proverbial sayings were collected by his disciples and pupils in a text called the *Analects for the Benefit of Posterity*. Both of these sage philosophers studied the lore and wisdom of the I Ching and used it in their philosophies. Confucius in particular is reputed to have developed a close and profound relationship with the I Ching in his latter years, and legend has it that he said if he was allowed another fifty years of life he would devote them to the study of the I Ching.

As an ancient book of wisdom, then, which inspired the most famous of Chinese philosophers and the enduring philosophies of Taoism and Confucianism, the philosophy that underpins or informs the I Ching is obviously important. It can be formulated as consisting of three main concepts or themes. The fundamental and basic idea that underpins everything else is the idea of change, the second fundamental theme is the theory of images, and the third crucial aspect of the I Ching are the Judgements.

Change

Change is the basis of the I Ching and of the universe. Confucius famously compared life and the process of change to a constantly flowing river. If one looks into a river one cannot fix one's attention on a fixed piece of river that stays the same and does not change. The river only exists as a constantly moving flow. So it is with time and change. One who is concerned with the meaning and significance of change does not focus his attention on individual things or situations, which are merely transitory. One concentrates on the river, on the eternal and unchanging principle that creates all change. This principle or law is the Tao of the philosopher Lao-Tse. The Tao is the one path, the way of all things. Everything is part of the one way. For this one way to come into being and influence it had to have a founding principle, a fixed point from which everything flows. This founding concept is called the 't'ai chi', originally meaning the ridge-pole. The ridge-pole or single line in itself represents oneness; but from this oneness all duality comes, for the single line also creates an above and a below, a right and a left, a front and a back. In other words we have the principle of opposition and a universe of opposites, from which all things and all meaning are created.

The originating polar opposites are known as the principles of yin and yang. They are also represented as the complementary light and dark parts of a circle.

Yin and yang are the two alternating primal states of being, their constant flowing into and changing into one another creating all the oppositions and all change in the universe. Change consists partly of the continuous transformation of one force into another, and partly as a cycle of change of pairs of complementary opposites in the world, such as night and day, summer and winter, heat and cold etc. All change is governed and given meaning by the universal law of the Tao.

Images, ideas and the senses

The second fundamental theme of the I Ching is the theory of images or underlying ideas. The eight founding and core trigrams of the I Ching are images of states of change, not of fixed situations or things. This is associated with the idea that all occurrences in the physical, known world are the representations or expressions of an original 'image' or 'idea' in the unknown, unseen world that underlies, and gives rise to, all know and perceived reality. (This is similar to, but not the same as, the Greek philosopher Plato's *Theory of Forms or Ideas*).

So everything that happens in this physical and visible world is just a representation of a 'real' event in the unseen and unknown world that lies beyond us and to which we, ordinarily, have no access. Also, the representation in this world which we perceive as an event in time, happens later in time that the 'real' event or idea; so the 'real' event is the origin in both the sense of 'being' and the sense of time.

Not everyone is denied access to this originating world beyond the ken of our ordinary senses. Holy men and wise men—sages—can gain entry to this mysterious and sacred realm or dimension. They are in direct contact with the higher sphere of the 'ideas' through the powers of their intuition; and from this perspective of insight and illumination they are in a position to intervene with authority and a wise decisiveness in human affairs. So wise men become not only mediators between heaven and earth, the two primal forces of yang and yin, they become like a third primal force in their ability and power to govern and shape events.

The I Ching, therefore, is in the position and function of a holy man or 'wise man', offering the benefits of its insight and wisdom to those who consult it. The I Ching, in its trigrams and hexagrams, is able to delineate the underlying states of change and show them through its images; it is also able to show the beginnings or birth of new and unfolding situations and events. This allows those who consult the I Ching to intervene with foresight and sagacity in the changing situations in their lives.

The Judgements

The third founding principle of the I Ching are the Judgements. The Judgements give expression in language to the images. They are able to articulate with prescient foreknowledge whether a given action in the present will have a future outcome that will be auspicious or inauspicious, bring good fortune or misfortune. The Judgements allow someone who consults the I Ching to make the decision to refrain from a course of action that seems favourable in the present but is liable to lead to future misfortune. So the consulter is not at the mercy of fate, not always the passive and suffering victim of its tyrannical whims and caprices.

The Judgements of the I Ching, along with the commentaries on them and interpretations of them, present to the interested and reflective reader a rich fund of ancient yet still relevant Chinese wisdom. In their breadth and depth the Judgements also allow the sagacious reader to consider and ponder the rich variety of human experience—to his own potential enrichment. Ideally, learning from his reading of the Judgements, the 'wise reader' will develop his own intuitive judgement and free will. These discerning and discriminating powers will help the 'wise reader' to mould the path of his life towards that of the one true path of the Tao. And thus the I Ching will have fulfilled its role and function as a book of wisdom.

Final points on the text

The quotations from the I Ching which are used in the text that accompanies each of the following hexagrams are taken from the Legge translation. In a few places the language has been modified to clarify its meaning; but otherwise the flavour and idiom of the original translation is preserved.

The Hsiang Chuan, or Image, of the Duke of Chou uses the recurring symbol of 'the dragon' in its analysis of the individual

lines of each hexagram. Legge provides this interpretation of the
symbolism of 'the dragon': " 'The dragon' is the symbol employed by the Duke of Chou to represent 'the superior man' and
especially 'the great man' exhibiting the virtues or attributes
characteristic of heaven [...] It has been from the earliest time
the emblem with the Chinese of the highest dignity and wisdom,
of sovereignty and sagehood, the combination of which consti-
tutes 'the great man' ".

The 'dragon' or 'superior man', 'great man' or 'wise man' are
analogous terms for an idealized state of perfect wisdom and
moral behaviour to which the 'ordinary man' must at all times
aspire. Each in his own way and to a different extent must try to
exemplify the virtues and moral strength of the 'wise man'. Either as a more or less enduring part of his character or as an aspect of his attitude and conduct in a specific situation, the ordinary man can strive to emulate, to attain and demonstrate, some
at least of the attributes and qualities of the 'wise man'—which
will include also accepting the responsibilities of such a position
and role. So that the ordinary man following a path of virtue and
honour can aspire to share at least temporarily in the respect and
honour accorded to the 'wise man'.

In the quotations from the Image and its line readings, the symbolism and terminology of 'the dragon' has been replaced here by
such phrases as 'the wise man' or the 'creative power' in order to
make the sense slightly more prosaic and referential than the
original symbolism. The intention being, simply, to make it easier
for the new and uninitiated reader to understand and grasp the
meanings and concepts that are being referred to.

As you read through and become acquainted with the text in
the hexagram system, please keep in mind that this book is a
guide to the I Ching—an accessible and useful means, it is hoped,
to forming an initial acquaintance with a text that can be fairly
daunting for a newcomer to it. This introductory text, though, is
not intended to be a substitute for the original full text of the I
Ching. If reading the unabridged version of the I Ching, one
would ponder the meaning of the text in the light of one's own
situation and decide whether to accept that it has a relevance and
practical meaning for that particular situation. Even more so for

this guide, then. The modern and occasionally simplified readings and interpretations of the quoted parts of the I Ching should not be taken as gospel, or the last word on the subject. Feel free to disagree with or dispute them in the light of your own reading and understanding of the quoted sections of the I Ching. Conversely, you should also be open to the possibility that the commentaries and interpretations of the hexagrams are saying something meaningful and relevant about you and your situation. You don't have to be afraid that having an open mind is the same as having a gullible mind. You will see, as you work through the texts of the hexagrams, that the I Ching makes it a cardinal virtue that at all times one retains one's integrity of mind and feeling.

When you have familiarized yourself sufficiently with this guide, you will then be in a position to do what was referred to in the introduction: make up your own mind as to the value of this text and by extension, the I Ching itself. At that point you can also make the decision whether to move on from this introductory text to a full and unabridged version of the I Ching. Whatever you decide it is hoped that this text will have adequately fulfilled its own limited remit and responsibility as a reliable guide.

Before you begin the process of consulting specific hexagrams for an answer to a specific question you have posed, it would probably be a good idea to read or skim through the whole chapter first, in order to familiarize yourself with the hexagrams and the style and format of the analysis and discussion of each hexagram. At the end of the chapter there is a section which deals with a sub-group of hexagrams called the sovereign hexagrams. Remember: when you do consult the hexagrams properly for the first time, make sure that the two hexagrams you have drawn have been correctly built from the bottom line upwards.

Hexagram 1
Ch'ien—The creative

Component Trigrams

Primary: Ch'ien—Heaven, creative (upper and lower). Nuclear: Ch'ien—Heaven, creative (upper and lower).

Keywords

Heaven, energy, creativity, action, perseverance, masculinity.

Commentary

This is an auspicious situation. A worthy goal is attained through the correct deployment of moral and spiritual energies. Continue with your intentions, as you will succeed because you have the energy, the desire and the resolve to do so. Your perseverance towards an outcome that will be right for you will ensure that things will unfold as you wish them. Beware of failure being snatched from the jaws of victory, though, because of overconfidence or trying to force the issue. Remain in patient harmony with your creativity and time will reward you by delivering your desired goal.

Judgement

The primary power is that which is great and originating, penetrating, advantageous, correct and firm.

Submit to the flow and let things take place in their own time. When anything ends something new begins, as the cycle of creativity continues.

Interpretation

The hexagram is complete and perfect yang with no yin lines. It is composed entirely of the Ch'ien trigram which represents heaven, creativity and energy; and in combination in upper and lower trigrams it signifies working in harmony with the pure energy and creativity of the universe

To achieve success in something worthwhile and morally good. Ch'ien also contains the concept of ceaseless movement and continual change, a never-ending process of evolution. The theme of the hexagram is change and transformation and this is embodied in the way that its six yang lines transform into their polar opposite in the six yin lines of K'un, Hexagram Two. Where Ch'ien is energy, K'un is form and the two together—like yin and yang—are necessary for creativity. Creativity and the form in which it manifests itself are inseparable.

Image

Heaven, in its motion: strength. The wise man nerves himself to ceaseless activity.

The transforming power of change is limitless, never-ending. Learn to develop, always move positively into the future. Stay strong and persevere and the help of 'heaven' and the power of creativity will bring you success.

Line readings

Line 1: *The creative power is lying hidden in the deep. It is not the time for active doing.*

Wait patiently and wisely for the right moment to commit yourself to action, to your plans. You will know it when it arrives. Don't try to anticipate it.

Line 2: *The creative power appears in the field. It will be advantageous to meet the great man.*

Things are beginning to happen. Look out for someone who can help you achieve your goal. A partnership at this time would be fruitful.

Line 3: *The wise man is active and vigilant all the day, and in the evening still careful and apprehensive. The position is dangerous, but there will be no mistake.*

Success and power also confer responsibilities. Behave prudently and maturely. Don't react to envy and don't get overconfident. Be aware of yourself and the effects of your influence but don't let this bring you down or make you anxious.

Line 4: *The creative power stirs and prepares to move, but remains hidden in the deep. There will be no mistake.*

Assess the situation for yourself and take the responsibility of deciding correctly whether it is the right time to move forward.

Line 5: *The creative power aligns with heaven. It will be advantageous to meet with the great man.*

Work in harmony with the power of change and creativity and you will become influential and attract other people of influence, to your benefit.

Line 6: *The creative power exceeds the proper limits. There will be occasion for repentance.*

Don't isolate yourself from others, become aloof in your time of success. Neither should you overreach yourself, entertain grandiose ideas about yourself or your ability. If you don't conduct yourself prudently and modestly you will bring on failure.

Hexagram 2
K'un—The receptive

Component Trigrams

Primary: K'un—receptive, earth (upper and lower). Nuclear: K'un—receptive, earth (upper and lower).

Keywords

Earth, form, yielding, gentleness, giving, obedience, femininity.

Commentary

The future holds promise for you but it may depend on others. Submit yourself to those you trust and who have your interests at heart. Be responsive to sound advice and follow it by acting appropriately. Have the necessary faith and strength to wait for your good fortune, but remain ready and responsive. Don't loose patience or become impulsive and seek to take the initiative or promote yourself and your interests. Adopt a quiet and patient resolution and be confident in the assurance that things will happen as you want them in time.

Judgement

The yielding power is that which is great and originating, penetrating, advantageous, correct and having the firmness of the mare. When the superior man has to make any movement, if he take the initiative, he will go astray; if he follow, he will find his proper lord. The advantageousness will be seen in his getting friends in the south-west, and losing friends in the north-east. If he rest in correctness and firmness, there will be good fortune.

The best, the wisest course at this time is to submit yourself to the influence and lead of trusted and respected others. This is passive strength. To take the initiative yourself would be rash and invite failure and confusion.

Interpretation

This hexagram is all yin, with no yang lines. It signifies subordination to the way of others, the wisdom of being passive and receptive; but it also indicates action and movement inspired by meditation and receptiveness to the currents of creative energy.

Solitary meditation and communing with your inner nature will lead to change and a new beginning. The hexagram is concerned with notions of physical space and acceptance of responsibility. This is demonstrated in the way it yields its own space by its own structure: the six yin lines change inevitably and naturally into the six yang lines of Ch'ien. This embodies the concept that creativity and the form in which it expresses itself are one.

Image

The earth is capacious and sustaining. The wise man, with his great virtue, supports men and things.

As you should live in harmony with the sustaining and protecting strength and power of the earth, so you should live in harmony with others and rely on their strength and support.

Line readings

Line 1: *One treads on hoarfrost. The strong ice will come soon.*

The supportive power of yin will soon help you if you keep going, but beware of being misled by unreliable or deceptive support.

Line 2: *Be true, calm and great; naturally done, it will be in every respect advantageous.*

Adopt the classic yin strengths and virtues of honesty, obedience to right authority, and calm perseverance. Don't succumb to transient doubt or misgiving.

Line 3: *Keep one's excellence under restraint, but firmly maintain it. If one should have occasion to engage in the king's service, one will not claim the success, but will bring affairs to a good issue.*

Quietly confident, you can continue in your chosen course without being deflected by the temptation to act prematurely. You can learn from other's example without feeling the need to attract attention to yourself or seek accolades.

Line 4: *Be like a tied sack. There will be no ground for blame or for praise.*

Protect yourself from harm by behaving prudently and cautiously. Keep your own counsel and maintain a quiet reserve.

Line 5: *Show a genuine humility. There will be great good fortune.*

Maintaining self-possession and a quiet decorum is the best and most fitting way to conduct yourself.

Line 6: *One tries to rule but only finds strife.*

By remaining wisely passive, and showing genuineness, loyalty and due obedience to wise and supportive sources of authority and help, you will be worthy of the benefits that will come your way. Don't be presumptuous or dismissive, otherwise you will only find failure. Be receptive and welcoming of change.

Hexagram 3
Chun—Initial adversity

Component Trigrams

Primary: K'an—water (upper). Chen—thunder (lower). Nuclear: Ken—mountain (upper), K'un—earth (below).

Keywords

Water, thunder, beginnings, immaturity, youth, inexperience.

Commentary

Possible opportunities can also be possible dangers. Be wary and remain alert. Trust and confidence in yourself and your chosen course, along with strength and determination, will be required to ensure that you will survive any potential hazards and initial difficulties. Then you can successfully move forward. Accept help if it is offered. Don't try to push things to a quick and successful conclusion: you could be running into a pit of failure. Take time to look, listen and learn.

Judgement

There will be great progress and success, and the advantage will come from being correct and firm. Any movement in advance should not be lightly undertaken. There will be advantage in appointing assistants.

Be prepared for problems and setbacks at the start of something new. These are only to be expected. Don't lose heart and don't give up. Enlist the support and help of others. Eventually, you will come out on the other side and find all is running smoothly.

Interpretation

This is a time of difficulty and danger, of chaotic circumstances and confusion. Thunder is a harbinger of dangerous conditions and water can also be hazardous to those who don't know the art of using it to support them, who can't swim to safety. There is tension in the air but this can also be an opportunity to learn and grow.

Image

Clouds and thunder. The wise man adjusts his measure of government as in sorting the threads of the warp and woof.

By maintaining a sense of balance and calm clear-sightedness during a period of disorder and confusion, being prepared to be flexible and resourceful also, you will guide yourself towards a haven of peace and good order.

Line readings

Line 1: *There is difficulty in advancing. It will be advantageous to remain correct and firm. Rule by serving will bring favour.*

Keep the faith and your patience even when you seem to be going nowhere, making no headway. Things will change. Be wise and economical in the use of your time and energy. Avoid conflict with others and seek their support to achieve your goal. Think about what you are doing but don't let this deflect you from progress towards your goal.

Line 2: *The young lady is distressed and obliged to return; even the horses of her chariot seem to be retreating. But she is not assailed by a lascivious man but by one who seeks her to be his wife. The young lady maintains her firm correctness, and declines a union. After ten years she will be united, and have children.*

This is a time for responding correctly and carefully to a tense and stressful situation. You should be in control of your destiny and have given careful thought to what you are doing and where you are going. Even genuine sources and offers of help should be treated with caution and circumspection, as they may lead to situations where things get out of hand, and especially out of your hands.

Line 3: *One follows the deer without the guidance of the forester, and finds oneself in the middle of the forest. The wise man, ac-*

quainted with the secret risks, thinks it better to give up the chase. If one goes forward, one will regret.

Trust and rely on your own instincts and judgement. If it seems foolish or risky to proceed, then don't.

Line 4: *The lady retreats with her horses and chariot. She seeks, however, the help of the one who seeks her to be his wife. Advance will be fortunate; all will turn out advantageously.*

Seize the day. Act when the moment seems ripe. Seek out partnerships to help you if any are available. Success will be yours.

Line 5: *There are difficulties in the way of dispensing the rich favours that are expected of one. With firmness and correctness there will be good fortune in small things. In great things there will be misfortune.*

Be alert to how you are affecting others, but don't let others' influence take over. Keep on your own way but take time to communicate with others, explain yourself and your aims. Don't brush others or their misunderstandings aside. Take them on board and move forward slowly until things are better.

Line 6: *One is obliged to retreat, weeping tears of blood in streams.*

An important time of choice. Somehow resolve the impasse you face, or turn away and start something new. The situation you are in cannot be allowed to stagnate. Take the initiative, one way or another.

Hexagram 4
Meng—Innocence

Component Trigrams

Primary: Ken—The Mountain (upper). K'an—Water (lower). Nuclear: K'un—Earth (above), Chen—Thunder (below).

Keywords

Ignorance, youthful folly, mountains, water, fog, misapprehension, instruction.

Commentary

You are inexperienced and lack wisdom. Retain your enthusiasm and determination but learn as you keep going. Something you thought was the case, may not in fact be the case. Don't let this annoy you. Keep calm and only act after careful and sensible thought. Scrutinize every aspect of the situation. Look back over everything you took for granted about the situation. Eventually the situation will become clearer and appear as it actually is, but this will only be achieved through your steady perseverance. Seek direction from someone more experienced and knowledgeable, who is able to give you wise advice and guidance. But don't substitute this help for your own efforts at self-development. Deepen your self-knowledge and learn to recognize and remedy your own folly.

Judgement

There will be progress and success. I do not go and seek the youthful and inexperienced, but he comes and seeks me. When he shows the sincerity that marks the first recourse to the oracle, I instruct him. If he apply a second and third time, that is troublesome; and I do not instruct the troublesome. There will be advantage in being firm and correct.

It is the role of the student to seek out the teacher, who will be waiting to be consulted. But the teacher will only respond to a respectful attitude and sensible questions. As a seeker after answers and guidance you must be respectful and give careful thought to your questions. This is the epitome of your position when you consult the I Ching.

Interpretation

This hexagram signifies youthful inexperience but also implies youthful success. It is auspicious for anyone engaged in something new, suggesting 'beginner's luck'. Let your beginner's enthusiasm and assurance carry you forward; but you should also endeavour to learn from others and your own experience as you go on. Otherwise your ignorance could have adverse consequences.

Image

A spring issuing forth from a mountain. The wise man strives to be resolute in his conduct and nourishes his virtue.

As you go on, strive always to learn and to gain increased clarity of mind and understanding. With perception and foresight comes a calm assurance which will be valuable in the future.

Line readings

Line 1: *One has to dispel ignorance. It will be advantageous to use punishment for that purpose, and to remove the shackles from the mind. But going on in punishment will give occasion for regret.*

Sometimes one can only learn through committing errors and facing the criticism and rebukes of others. If the criticism is justified and fair, then it should be accepted and learned from. Develop your own powers of self-criticism and self-discipline but don't let them inhibit you or hold you back.

Line 2: *To exercise forbearance with the ignorant will bring good fortune.*

It will be to your credit and advantage to deal kindly and patiently with those who, like you, are inexperienced and lacking in knowledge.

Line 3: *When a woman sees a man of wealth she will not keep her person from him, and in no way will advantage come from her.*

Don't let your respect and admiration for another turn into a dangerous idolatry. Never lose your sense of yourself and your own worth and the responsibilities you owe to yourself. Neither should you become closely associated with someone you are not compatible with.

Line 4: *One is bound in chains of ignorance. There will be occasion for regret.*

Don't respond to difficulties arising from your inexperience by daydreams, compensatory fantasy and escapism. You will only make things more difficult for yourself. Dreams are for the sleeping mind; keep your waking mind on the real world.

Line 5: *One is a simple youth without experience. There will be good fortune.*

Sometimes good luck can attend innocence and simplicity. Youthful optimism should be retained, as well as a modest sense of one's limitations and abilities. An inflated sense of oneself should be deflated as soon as one perceives it.

Line 6: *One punishes the ignorant youth. But no advantage will come from doing him an injury. Advantage would come from warding off injury from him.*

Mistakes must be recognized and learned from, but there is no need to make an issue of them or to wallow in them—whether they belong to you or to another inexperienced person. This is a waste of time and energy, which creates difficulty and disorder. Deal sensibly with mistakes by accepting them as moments or opportunities of learning, then put them behind and move on.

Hexagram 5
Hsu—Waiting

Component Trigrams

Primary: K'an—Water (upper), Ch'ien—Heaven (lower). Nuclear: Li—Fire (above), Tui—Marshes (below).

Keywords

Sustenance, water, heaven, patience, nourishment, light, perseverance.

Commentary

Carry on honestly and sincerely with the tasks at hand, and be patient with regard to your attainment of your real goal. Wait for the most favourable moment before trying to advance your plans; only when the right circumstances and resources are in place will it be propitious to act and move on. Then it will be possible to attain your goal. In the meantime cultivate patience and self-control. Don't try to force things. If you concentrate on those areas of your life that offer the greatest possibility of continuity, then you will be doing the right thing. Don't expect others to help before the moment is right. Otherwise you will only create difficulty and risk failure. Keep in good spirits. You will eventually attain your desired goal.

Judgement

With sincerity, there will be brilliant success. With firmness there will be good fortune; and it will be advantageous to cross the great stream.

Remain determined and committed to your course, but pause
and take time out. Use it as an opportunity for a period of reflection and taking stock of yourself and your plans. Get things into a
realistic perspective. Continue to have faith in yourself.

Interpretation

The K'an trigram represents danger, and this is an obstacle to the
strength and creative energy of Ch'ien. Strength could confront
this danger and struggle with it; but the best plan is to bide one's
time and wait for the most propitious moment. This hexagram is
about self-discipline. Calmness and self-restraint are the keys to
success. There are streams which must be crossed but now is not
the right time. You must have the strength and patience to wait for
the right moment to cross the stream.

Image

Clouds ascending to heaven. The wise man eats and drinks, feasts
and enjoys himself as if there were nothing else to employ him.

Be content and happy with what you have in the present. Soon,
new growth will be possible when the clouds deliver the nourishing rain. In the meantime enjoy the moment for what it has.

Line readings

Line 1: *One waits in the distant border. It will be well for one to
constantly maintain the purpose thus shown, in which case there
will be no error.*

Keep your mind calmly on the present moment while you wait
for some trouble to arrive. Its shape and timing is outside your
control so concentrate on what is in your control, but remain
ready to deal with whatever comes. You will know it when it arrives and with self-possession and calmness you will be able to
cope successfully with whatever challenges it brings.

Line 2: *One waits on the sand of the mountain stream. One will
suffer the small injury of being spoken against, but in the end
there will be good fortune.*

You may be isolated as the scapegoat for something that goes
wrong, and have to face general censure and disapproval. Let it
wash over you and don't censure or blame those who find a convenient scapegoat in you. There may be upsetting gossip but do

not respond to it. Keep your peace and your counsel. Eventually, things will turn out well for you.

Line 3: *One is in mud close by the stream. One thereby invites the approach of injury.*

Faced with worrying difficulty, your anxiety has caused you to act too soon and made the situation worse. Avoid any further complications and trouble by stopping where you are and being prudent and cautious while you wait.

Line 4: *One is waiting in the place of blood. But one will get out of the cavern.*

You can do nothing about a situation and feel trapped. Keep calm and accept this as how it was meant to be.

Line 5: *One is waiting amidst the trappings of a feast. Through firmness and correction there will be good fortune.*

Take the opportunity of a brief distraction from your troubles and enjoy the pleasures that are on offer to you. But don't be tempted by them into forgetting that you have to continue in your journey. Use this time as a welcome respite that will allow you to gather strength for going on.

Line 6: *One is in the cavern. But there are three guests coming, without being urged, to one's help. If one receives them respectfully there will be good fortune in the end.*

Your may run into trouble or an impasse in your plans or in your direction towards your hoped-for goal. Have faith in other people and remain open to help from them. Your trust in others will be rewarded. Things may not turn out as you wished but you will be able to move on with little loss.

Hexagram 6
Sung—Conflict

Component Trigrams

Primary: Ch'ien—Heaven (upper), K'an—Water (lower). Nuclear: Sun—Wind (above), Li—Fire (below).

Keywords

Strength, danger, stormy waters, obstruction, caution.

Commentary

You find your strength and your direction bringing you into a situation of conflict with others. Don't pour fuel onto the fire by trying to oppose and overcome the obstacles before you. If you fall into the temptation of seeking to win by using your strength and force this will only provoke the same force being used against you. Conflict is useless, a waste of time and energy. The urge to win is a false goal and a distraction. Withdraw and remain aloof from dispute and contention. It is the wise and politic thing to do. Seek compromise and accommodation with others. Listen to criticism and take advice.

Judgement

Though there is sincerity in one's contention, yet one will meet with opposition and obstruction; but if one cherish an apprehensive caution, there will be good fortune. If, though, one perseveres with the contention to the bitter end, there will be evil. It will be advantageous to see the great man; it will not be advantageous to cross the great stream.

You are stuck in a state of stagnant conflict through your insistence that everyone should always concede to the justness and rightness of your case; everyone else is wrong and you are always right. You have to concede that this is not the case and be prepared to meet others halfway. Follow the advice of an objective judge. In the meantime, it is not an auspicious time to start anything new.

Interpretation

In the structure of the hexagram, the upper primary trigram signifies strength and energy; the lower one denotes danger. There is a danger from outside is the suggestion, and this will lead to confrontation. The theme of the hexagram is conflict. Sometimes conflict cannot be avoided; but then it must be dealt with properly. Aggression will not solve things. Develop the ability to negotiate with others and seek a rapport with them. Pay heed and respect to sound and authoritative advice. Avoid getting involved in anything that takes you out of your depth.

Image

Heaven and water moving away from each other. The wise man, in the transaction of affairs, takes good counsel about his first steps.

Make this a period of inner communing and meditation about the imminent new beginning; but don't act on your intentions yet.

Line readings

Line 1: *One is not perpetuating the matter of contention. One will suffer the small injury of being spoken against, but the end will be fortunate.*

At the moment when it seems conflict is about to begin you should pull back and pull away from the other person. Don't worry about what is initially said regarding this action, as it will all come out right in the end.

Line 2: *One is unequal to the contention. One should retire; one will fall into no mistake.*

This continues the salutary advice of the previous line. Your calm withdrawal from the situation will benefit everyone, but especially yourself.

Line 3: *Firmly correct, one keeps in the old place assigned for one's support. Perilous as the position is, there will be good fortune in the end. Should one engage in the king's business, one will not claim the merit of achievement.*

Continue learning the traditional wisdom that you have judiciously and successfully been acting upon. Let your old ways stay in the past. Don't take on any new work or responsibilities from your employer.

Line 4: *One is unequal to the contention. One returns to a study of heaven's ordinances, and rests in being firm and correct. There will be good fortune.*

Be firm but flexible, so that if your strength and purpose brings you up against someone who initiates conflict, you can calmly walk away. Be resolute in this and everything will turn out for the best.

Line 5: *One is contending, and with great good fortune.*

Put your faith in an objective third party to provide a fair assessment and good advice. If you are sincere and in the right then you will benefit accordingly.

Line 6: *One has the leather belt of reward conferred by the king, and thrice shall it be taken away in the morning.*

Don't get overconfident in the first flush of success. Where there has been one conflict there will be more.

Hexagram 7
Shih—The army

Component Trigrams

Primary: K'un—Earth (upper), K'an—Water (lower). Nuclear: K'un—Earth (above), Chen—Thunder (below)

Keywords

Earth, water, firmness, authority, group action, danger, dissension, devotion.

Commentary

There is a lack of harmony in your present situation, with contending forces causing confusion and unrest. But if you show firmness of purpose and keep your eye steadily on a goal which is worthy of attainment then you will succeed. Your exemplary action will transform aimless confusion into coordination and a worthwhile sense of direction. You will be an inspiration and a guide to others and will command their respect and admiration. With their help and support you will attain a position of distinction.

Judgement

With firmness and correctness and a leader of age and experience, there will be good fortune and no error.

A group of soldiers requires a steady and competent leader to unite them and keep them in good order. The leader must eliminate grievance and injustice and ensure instead that justice and peaceful concord prevail in the group. In and through this leadership endeavour he will command the respect, loyalty and love of his soldiers. The implication is that you should recruit the enthusiastic help and support of those around you to work together for a worthwhile common goal.

Interpretation

The only solid line in the hexagram is found in the middle line of the lower primary trigram. This gives rise to the image of a general who is the commander of the broken yin lines. This hexagram is about proper discipline, good order and legitimate and worthy power. It shows that an effective army requires effective soldiers and leadership. The good army remains in a state of prepared readiness until action is necessary, when it responds with spirit and alacrity. In a situation of conflict there is always the possibility of civil insurrection, but if the people are treated properly they will contribute to the size of the army.

Image

Water in the midst of the earth. The wise ruler nourishes and educates the people and collects from among them the multitude of his army.

A ruler must instil a respect and desire for justice, good authority and harmony in his people by his own merits and example, commanding love and respect for his kindness, strength and unstinting support.

Line readings

Line 1: *The army goes forth according to the proper rules. If these not be good there will be misfortune.*

Success depends on the right motivation and the best preparation. Take a good and honest look at yourself.

Line 2: *The leader is in the middle of the army. There will be good fortune and no error. The king has thrice conveyed to him the orders of his favour.*

You are awarded a distinction which is merited by the respect those around you have for your good judgement and successful work. They share in the credit and honour, as you all work together in a situation of mutual respect.

Line 3: *The army may have many inefficient leaders. There will be misfortune.*

Be honest and vigilant about your faults and weaknesses otherwise your endeavour will end in failure. Maintain a perceptive and judicious sense of authority and control over yourself and others.

Line 4: *The army is in retreat. There is no error.*

Now is the time to make a tactical retreat from a situation. You are not capitulating but surviving to fight again another day. Wait until a more advantageous time arrives. Be patient.

Line 5: *There are birds in the fields which it will be advantageous to seize and destroy. There will be no error. If the oldest son leads the army, and younger men idly occupy offices assigned to them, then however firm and correct he may be, there will be misfortune.*

Success requires maturity. You must compensate for the immaturity of yourself and your advisers by seeking out those who can give wise and mature guidance. Guard against the mistake of confusing age with wisdom.

Line 6: *The king gives his rewards, appointing some to be rulers of states, and others to undertake the headship of clans; but small men should not be employed.*

You have achieved success but don't bask unthinkingly in your moment of glory. You should take time to survey and assess the nature and merits of your attainment with a scrupulous honesty. Ask yourself if you are where you deserve to be and where you want to be, and whether you are better, morally and practically, than the person you have replaced. Be true to yourself.

Hexagram 8
Pi—Union

Component Trigrams
Primary: K'an—Water (upper), K'un— Earth (lower). Nuclear: Ken—The Mountain (above), K'un—Earth (below).

Keywords
Water, earth, cooperation, sound relationships, alliance, unity.

Commentary
You are in a favourable situation for strengthening the bonds you already have with your chosen associates, joining together for your mutual support and benefit. You will be able to consolidate your already good position by doing this. Your success in achieving your goal depends on harmonious alliance and well-planned cooperative effort. You must be worthy, though, of others' com-

mitment to your interests. Don't fall into the error of thinking that your status and power means that you can do what you like, in terms of yourself and other people. With the support and confidence of the right people, allied to your own sincere commitment and determination, you are in a favourable position to achieve success if you act now. The best and fairest leader ensures the right forms of cooperative action to bring about creative progress in the community. That wise leader also knows that it is his honesty and sincerity which is the binding and decisive factor in the success of the situation, and is the true measure of his own success.

Judgement

In union there is good fortune. But let one re-examine oneself, as if consulting an oracle, and see whether one's virtue be great, unremitting and firm. If it be so, there will be no error. Those who have not rest will then come to one; and with those who are too late in coming it will be ill.

You must decide if you have the strength to enter into a long-term partnership with someone you have a common bond with. Your cannot dither over this decision or you risk it being summarily withdrawn.

Interpretation

In the structure of the trigrams, water lies on the earth. Water merges with the earth and they become one. The theme here is harmony. The hexagram emphasizes success deriving from harmonious and beneficial union. It has to be brought about by a leader who maintains a consistent virtue appropriate to his status and power. And this proper authority promotes union as it is communicated successively to those in responsible positions of power and influence. Anyone with whom you feel a strong bond is someone who will be able to give you help when you need it, but if your intuition does not support this then it is not the right time.

Image

Water flowing over the earth. The ancient kings established the various states and maintained an affectionate relation to their princes.

You should form close relationships with others in your group and make sure that your goals are their goals also, because only by working together for common aims will the group attain them.

Line readings

Line 1: *One seeks by sincerity to attain one's goal. There will be no error. Let the breast be full of sincerity as an earthenware vessel is of its contents, and it will in the end bring other advantages.*

Be sincere in all that you do and make sure you are in sympathy with others. Be prepared to be flexible and accommodating.

Line 2: *One moves towards union and attachment that comes from the inward mind. With firm correctness there will be good fortune.*

You must be true to yourself and others. Don't be false to your own self and direction just to try and remain in harmony with others.

Line 3: *One is seeking for union with such people as one ought not to be associated with.*

You are involved with a group that is wrong for you and must withdraw. Otherwise you will be unable to freely form other friendships in the future. Maintain some friendly contact with the group after you leave it if it makes the process easier.

Line 4: *One seeks for union with the one beyond oneself. With firm correctness there will be good fortune.*

You can freely reveal and express your thoughts and feelings, remembering to remain true to yourself and in touch with your own direction and goals.

Line 5: *The king urges the pursuit of the game in three directions only, and allows the escape of the animals before him. The people of his towns do not prevent it. There will be good fortune.*

Only those who chose to be a part of your group, should be. Coercing someone into to it, or to remain in it if they don't want to, is wrong.

Line 6: *One seeks union and attachment without having taken the first step towards such an end. There will be misfortune.*

Seize the day. Delay can be fatal. Decide what you want to do and do it straight away.

Hexagram 9
Hsiao Ch'u—Taming power

Component Trigrams

Primary: Sun—Wind (upper), Ch'ien— Heaven (lower). Nuclear: Li—Fire (above), Tui —Marsh (below).

Keywords

Restraining power of the small, wind, heaven, patience, strength, yielding.

Commentary

Tame any urge to force your way past obstacles in your path. Self-control and restraint can be more formidable and effective than aggressive force. It is better at this time to cultivate your inner strengths and outer qualities. By so doing you will dissolve away or outlast your present obstacles. Be strong in yourself and be gentle and kind to others. With faith and trust in yourself you will be able to survive any temporary setbacks in good spirits. If you try to take short-term advantage of a situation, or if you act arrogantly with others, then you will bring trouble down upon yourself.

Judgement

There will be progress and success. We see dense clouds, but no rain coming from our borders in the west.

This hexagram concerns strength with gentleness. You will be able to move some temporary obstacles from your path by being congenial to others while remaining true to yourself and your aims.

Interpretation

The solitary broken line is in a position of great influence, and great power is being held under restraint. The humble and yielding element in the hexagram holds sway for the time being. You may not be going forward at the moment but everything is auspicious for success. This will be achieved by consolidating outward strengths of reciprocal respect and amicable relations with others while remaining steadfast to your inner self and goals.

Image

The wind moves in the sky. The wise man adorns the outward manifestation of his virtue.

Use this fallow period in the advancement of your plans as an opportunity to assess how you present yourself to others and how you behave towards them, making any adjustments and improvements that you feel are necessary.

Line readings

Line 1: *One returns and pursues one's own course. What mistake should one fall into? There will be good fortune.*

If you are unable to achieve your goals just now then it is best to walk away from the situation.

Line 2: *One returns to the proper course. There will be good fortune.*

Consider following the example of others who have retreated from similar goals to yours.

Line 3: *The supporting strap has been removed from the carriage. A husband and wife look on each other with averted eyes.*

Restrain your aggression and your forceful attempts to coerce people into your way of thinking. Continuing to try and push yourself forward against the obstacles that confront you will result in failure.

Line 4: *One is sincere. The danger of bloodshed is thereby averted, and the ground for apprehension dismissed. There will be no mistake.*

Follow the example of those prescient others who are aware that circumstances are changing: act now without delay.

Line 5: *One is sincere and draws others to unite around one. Rich in resources, one employs one's neighbours in the same cause as oneself.*

Your are well-matched with those you are in partnership with and this augurs well for the future. You are fortunate in your friendships.

Line 6: *The rain has fallen, and it is time for the onward progress to stop. One values the fullness of one's achievement and virtue. But weakness that has achieved such a result, if it plumes itself upon it, will be in a position of peril and like the full moon, which must now wane. When the wise man attains his end, he remains in quiet.*

Be alert and wary when you are on the point of success. Take nothing for granted and be careful that you aren't getting into something that will feel like a trap.

Hexagram 10
Lu—Stepping

Component Trigrams

Primary: Ch'ien—Heaven (upper), Tui—Marsh (lower). Nuclear: Sun—Wind (above), Li—Fire (below).

Keywords

Sky, marsh, propriety, courtesy, purpose, degree, order, caution.

Commentary

Don't hold back, but move onward swiftly with confidence. This hexagram is about harmony between the small and the great. When you achieve good relationships with those above and below you then you ensure that anything is within your grasp. Remain correct in your dealings with others, showing due deference and generous forbearance where appropriate. Make sure that you have the support of influential people in your undertakings. This will be of more benefit in achieving your aims than any impetuous initiatives of your own. Beware of incurring the disfavour of someone in authority by behaving rashly.

Judgement

One treads on the tail of a tiger, which does not bite one. There will be progress and success.

Despite difficulties, your proper conduct towards others and your inner strength will take you onwards to success.

Interpretation

This hexagram has joy below strength and indicates that there will be a fortunate ending to a period of danger. This is achieved through the observance of proper conduct in oneself and toward others. Learn to work harmoniously with others, despite dispari-

ties in status, and achieve success together. Don't be aloof and
rude to those to whom you should be generously offering your
attention and support.

Image

Heaven above, the waters of the marsh below. The wise man discriminates between high and low, and gives settlement to the
aims of the people.

   Though some people are at higher levels in the hierarchy of
power and influence they do not discriminate against those below
them. There is mutual respect.

Line readings

Line 1: *One treads one's accustomed path. If one goes forward,
there will be no error.*

   You have the choice of accepting or rejecting favourable opportunities for your progress which will be offered to you.

Line 2: *One treads the path that is light and easy in quiet and
solitude. If one is firm and correct, there will be good fortune.*

   Your way is clear and untroubled, so don't be tempted to stray
off your path into conflicts with others who are having troubles.

Line 3: *A one-eyed man thinks he can see. A lame man thinks he
can walk well. One treads on the tail of a tiger and is bitten. All
this indicates ill fortune. There is a mere braggart and fool acting
the part of a great ruler.*

   Don't be presumptuous or complacent about your situation,
keep a sharp look-out. Otherwise you will fail.

Line 4: *One treads on the tail of a tiger. One becomes full of apprehensive caution. In the end there will be good fortune.*

   Although things may be difficult there is cause for hope and
optimism. Remain cautious but determined and you will overcome the problems that you face.

Line 5: *One has a resolute tread. But though one is firm and correct, there will be peril.*

   You should continue in your path with determination but anticipate and be prepared for further difficulties along the way.

Line 6: *One should look at the whole course one has trodden, and
examine what the evidence tells. If it be complete and without
failure, there will be great good fortune.*

From your position of achievement it is now time to assess what you have done and compare it with what you set out to do. This is important as others will judge you by end results and how you achieved them, not by initial motives.

Hexagram 11
T'ai—Tranquility

Component Trigrams
Primary: K'un—Earth (upper), Ch'ien—Heaven (lower). Nuclear: Chen—Thunder (above), Tui—Marsh (below).

Keywords
Earth, heaven, harmony, union, cooperation, prosperity, beginnings.

Commentary
Everything in the situation is favourable. It is all going as it should for you. It is a good time for a successful new undertaking. Harmony and cooperation are the means to success. Join together with others in a shared endeavour to achieve a common goal. Your selfless aspirations will be supported and guided by worthwhile and influential people. But if you are selfish or insincere then you will fail. Having finally achieved success, you must then ready yourself for dangerous challenges and difficulties.

Judgement
We see the little gone and the great come. There will be good fortune, with progress and success.

It is possible for anyone to develop the strength of a calm demeanour if they want to. A sense of contentment then follows and everything is rendered harmonious.

Interpretation
This hexagram shows three yielding, yin lines leaving and three strong, yang lines approaching. This suggests the onset of a favourable and successful time. Your whole situation is harmonious and in good order. The calmness and strength within you is reflected by the benign peace around you.

Image

Heaven and earth in communication together. The wise ruler, in harmony with this, fashions and completes his regulations after the courses of the heavens and the earth, and assists the applications of the adaptations furnished by them, in order to benefit the people.

As the farmer works in harmony with the seasons to provide for his needs, so the wise and sensible person progresses by working with nature and not against it.

Line readings

Line 1: *When grass is pulled up it brings with it other stalks with whose roots it is connected. One's advance will be fortunate.*

Others with the same aims as you will want to join with you, and you should welcome them on board.

Line 2: *One is forbearing with the uncultivated; one can cross the river without a boat; one does not forget the distant; one has no selfish friendships. Thus does one prove oneself acting in accordance with the course of the due Mean. Forbearing; resolved; vigilant; impartial.*

Showing forbearance, being resourceful and determined, being vigilant, and being selfless and impartial in relations with others: these are the four principal ways of overcoming difficulties, which you should adopt for all undertakings in your life.

Line 3: *While there is no state of peace that is not liable to be disturbed, and no departure of evil men that will not be followed by their return, yet when one is firm and correct, and accepts that disorder may occur, one will commit no error. There is no occasion for sadness at the certainty of such recurring changes; and in this mood the happiness of the present may be long enjoyed.*

Things are always changing so you must expect bad fortune to follow good. Accept this as natural and you will be able to fully savour the present favourable moment.

Line 4: *One does not rely on one's own rich resources but goes down to meet one's neighbours. They all come, not because they have received warning, but in the sincerity of their hearts.*

You should have an inner confidence and contentment from your justified success, and therefore have no need to adopt vain-

glorious displays of conduct and behaviour in order to impress or in-
timidate others with your success. Be sincere and at ease with others.

Line 5: *The king's younger sister marries and humbly serves her
husband. By such a course there is happiness and there will be
great good fortune.*

Be modest and sincere.

Line 6: *The city wall falls into the moat. It is not the time to use
the army. The ruler may announce his orders to the people of his
own city; but however correct and firm he may be, he will have
cause for regret.*

Because you have not integrated all aspects of your life into a
strong and harmonious whole then the inevitable change is coming into your vulnerable life. You have no choice but to accept
what happens. A passive, stoic patience is now required.

Hexagram 12
P'i—Stagnation

Component Trigrams

Primary: Ch'ien—Heaven (upper), K'un—Earth (lower). Nuclear: Sun—Wind (above), Ken—The Mountain (below).

Keywords

Standstill, obstruction, disharmony, disunion, lack of cooperation, lack of means, deterioration.

Commentary

This is not an auspicious time. You have been going in the wrong
direction and now you are faced with a testing time of struggle
and disorder. You may be cut-off from someone close or deprived
of the pleasure of something in your life. There may be unworthy
people in positions of influence who will take against you. Things
will get worse before they get better. But eventually, get better
they will. In the meantime you should not begin anything new.
You must wait patiently for favourable circumstances to return.
Face and accept your fate with quiet fortitude and a firm resolve
not to let it prevent you from finding your way back to your true
path and moving forward again. If you remain steadfast in this

way you will find the troubles will clear and you will be able to
see a happier time approaching.

Judgement

There is a lack of good understanding between the different
classes of men. This is unfavourable to the firm and correct
course of the wise man. We see the great gone and the little come.

You are surrounded by disruption and confusion. Withdraw if
necessary. The important thing now is to remain true to yourself.
You may become the focus for malign intent by some. The only
thing to do is stay out of their way.

Interpretation

Three strong yang lines are leaving, three yielding yin lines are
approaching. The situation is the reverse of hexagram 11. It is not
an auspicious time. There will be trouble and disorder. The favourable period of development has reached its climax and the
forces of decline and dissolution are taking over.

Image

Heaven and earth are not in intercommunication. The wise man
restrains the manifestation of his virtue, and avoids the calamities
that threaten him. There is no opportunity of conferring on him
the glory of reward.

Don't be lured into anything merely because you have been se-
duced by its glamorous appeal.

Line readings

Line 1: *Grass pulled up brings with it the other stalks with whose
roots it is connected. With firm correctness there will be good fortune and progress.*

Sometimes you have to withdraw from an adverse situation in
order to preserve your energies for better future circumstances.

Line 2: *Patience and obedience for the small man brings good
fortune. If the great man is patient and obedient in the face of distress and obstruction, he will have success.*

Sometimes it is necessary to be involved with materialist people but you have successfully remained aloof from their influence
and have been faithful to yourself. You should continue in this
course.

Line 3: *One is ashamed of one's hidden purpose.*

Those who have prospered through unfair means cannot hide this fact from themselves. If this refers to you then you should act accordingly on that shame and return to a truer path.

Line 4: *One acts in accordance with the command of heaven, and commits no error. One's companions will come and share in one's happiness.*

You must employ authority in order to proceed. Others will come to help you and share in your success.

Line 5: *One brings the distress and obstruction to a close. But continue to be cautious.*

As obstruction disappears and you begin to move forward you should be vigilant for unlooked-for and unexpected setbacks. Exercise caution, curb any tendency to complacency and presumption.

Line 6: *Distress and obstruction are removed. Now there will be joy.*

New progress is beginning, with some help from others. The outlook is promising.

Hexagram 13
T'ung jen—Fellowship

Component Trigrams

Primary: Ch'ien—Heaven (upper), Li—Fire. Nuclear: Ch'ien—Heaven (above), Sun—Wind (below).

Keywords

Heaven, fire, coherence, union, victory in numbers, like-mindedness.

Commentary

You should involve yourself in a union with others to achieve the worthiest of aims. Be guided by your intuition about the goals to aim for. Everyone should strive in their allotted tasks to achieve a mutually beneficial outcome, otherwise the undertaking will fail. You should commit yourself unselfishly and in the spirit of true kinship to this communal endeavour. If you are able to remain true to yourself and do not arrogantly insist you are right in the event of disputes arising, then you will gain great reward. Act with prudence and good judgement, and be respectful to the thoughts and feelings, and success will be yours.

Judgement

We see the union of men out in the open: progress and success. It will be advantageous to cross the great stream. It will be advantageous to maintain the firm correctness of the wise man.

Mutual success depends on your clear-sightedness, a firm commitment to your goal, and true kinship with others.

Interpretation

The hexagram has fire mounting upwards to the heavens. Things are moving in the right direction. It is the yielding yin line in this hexagram which holds the seemingly stronger yang lines together. The hexagram is the complement of Shih or The Army. The union which is promoted here must be out in the open, clear and honest. It will be achieved and held together because of worthiness of character and not because of status or influence. A union bonded with love and respect will be capable of withstanding the greatest of afflictions, but it will still require to exercise a due caution and circumspection.

Image

Heaven and fire. The wise man distinguishes things according to their kinds and classes.

Nothing can function without good order. If there is anything which needs putting into some kind of order then now is the time to do it. This could include looking at relationships.

Line readings

Line 1: *The union of men comes through an open gate. There will be no regret.*

Be open and honest with those you have bonded together with to achieve a common goal.

Line 2: *One joins in with one's kindred. There will be occasion for regret.*

You limit your potential by restricting yourself to a small circle of friends. Open up to a wider circle of companionship.

Line 3: *One stands on top of a high mound, and hides one's arms in the thick grass. But for three years one makes no demonstration.*

You are not yet fully and unselfishly committed to the aims and individuals of the group you are a member of. This is the case with others as well. There is an awareness of all this which has resulted in mutual suspicion and a lack of honesty. It would be better for you to withdraw a little. It will take much time for you and this group to accept one another.

Line 4: *One is mounted on the city wall; but does not proceed to make the attack that one has contemplated. There will be good fortune.*

Your belief that there was conflict in the group was false. You have misjudged the situation and the others in the group and are feeling suitably chagrined at yourself. This is a salutary experience as it imparts the lesson that you cannot always be right.

Line 5: *One first wails and cries out, and then laughs. The great army conquers, and men meet together.*

Although you sometimes feel isolated in the group you are a valuable member of what is a strong and coherent group with many common bonds. Don't brood but simply accept the satisfying responsibilities of being a member.

Line 6: *One is in the suburbs. There will be no occasion for repentance.*

You should promote the case for a common humanity by seeking to create bonds with those different from you, trying to find common cause with them.

Hexagram 14
Ta Yu—Possessing plenty

Component Trigrams

Primary: Li—Fire (upper, Ch'ien—Heaven (lower). Nuclear: Tui—Marsh (above), Ch'ien—Heaven (below).

Keywords

Fire, heaven, abundance, prosperity, rectitude, supreme good fortune.

Commentary

It is a time of great achievement and prosperity for you when your circumstances will significantly improve. You will attain your goal with a surprising lack of difficulty. Your best qualities are made obvious to all, and your actions are characterized by an obvious integrity and worthiness. You are the fortunate beneficiary of support and help from powerful and influential people. Make sure you don't treat them or their help lightly or abuse it by failing to grasp the opportunities before you.

Judgement

There will be great progress and success.

When the ruler possesses the qualities of firmness and strength, clear-sightedness and a sense of order, and they are combined in effective harmony, then he will be accorded honour.

Interpretation

Fire above the heavens: everything is now clear, evil is overwhelmed and the forces of good prosper and advance. This hexagram indicates, directly and positively, that this is an exceptionally auspicious time for you. All of the trigrams, both primary and nuclear, signify rising. It indicate a period of great prosperity and good fortune. The only thing that could possibly interfere with this is stupid self-pride and selfishness. In the hexagram a benevolent ruler is supported by able and willing helpers. His modesty and unselfishness enables him to see with clarity the need for harmony with others.

Image

Light in the heavens. The wise man represses what is evil and gives distinction to what is good, in sympathy with the excellent heaven-conferred nature.

We should all strive to emulate the wise man who conquers evil and establishes the power of good.

Line readings

Line 1: *There is no approach to what is injurious, and there is no error. Let there be a realization of the difficulty and danger of the position and there will be no error to the end.*

Guard against sacrificing your integrity for the sake of gaining power and possessions. Tendencies to arrogance and pomposity must be eliminated before you are faced with imminent difficulties.

Line 2: *A large wagon carrying its load. In whatever direction advancement be made, there will be no error.*

You must show flexibility and not become a slave to your possessions. Be prepared to move if necessary and be open to the willing help of others.

Line 3: *A prince presents his offerings to heaven. A small man would be unequal to such a duty.*

To give is better than to receive. Hoarded wealth and possessions will stifle your potential. You must share your good fortune with others.

Line 4: *One keeps one's resources under restraint. There will be no error.*

Don't be envious of others and don't show-off to others. Be modest and composed within yourself.

Line 5: *One is sincere with others, who in return are sincere also. Let one display a proper majesty, and there will be good fortune.*

Don't let the sense of your own dignity blind you to others. Don't stand on your own self-importance but reciprocate others' unselfish offers of friendship.

Line 6: *One is accorded help from heaven. There will be good fortune, advantage in every respect.*

A sincere, modest and honourable person has been duly rewarded by heaven for his faith and outstanding qualities. If you meet such a person share in his good fortune and learn from his example.

Hexagram 15
Ch'ien—Humility

Component Trigrams

Primary: K'un—Earth (upper), Ken—The Mountain (lower).
Nuclear: Chen—Thunder (above), K'an—Water (below).

Keywords

Earth, the mountain, compensation, obedience, sincerity, generosity.

Commentary

A favourable situation awaits you if remain modest and worthy. You must cultivate these virtues for their own sake and this will offset any possible faults you develop. Adopting this course will bring you to success. By respecting and honouring others you increase your strength and worthiness for success. To be humble, though, does not mean to be abject; you should be prepared to challenge and speak out against evil in others if you find it. Your prospects for enduring success are good but only if you attain the strength to be consistent and sincere in your humility.

Judgement

There will be progress and success. The wise man being humble will have a good outcome from his undertakings.

Those who brag about themselves and disdain others, those who scorn others and show disrespect towards them, will win no friends and gain no help and support. A good person, who is humble, honest and sincere in dealings with others, is a worthy person. Model yourself on the good person.

Interpretation

In the hexagram the single yang line—the third line— is strong but it humbles itself. The earth is raised to a superior position. You should cultivate the virtue of modesty in all sincerity, with no ulterior motives. Be humble in your relations and dealings with others. Thus will you overcome any tendencies towards pride and disrespect for others. Balance is required. The means is modesty and humility; their discipline is endless. You must ceaselessly strive to cultivate them if you wish to grow in strength and worthiness of character.

Image

A mountain in the midst of the earth. The wise man diminishes what is excessive in himself, and increases where there is any defect, bringing about an equality, according to the nature of the case, in his treatment of himself and others.

Balance and compromise, disdaining extremes, are the wise positions to attain.

Line readings

Line 1: *A wise man adds humility to humility. Even the great stream may be crossed with this, and there will be good fortune.*

If you are humble and sincere, and in harmony with others, then you can confidently tackle difficult undertakings, assured of success. But if you are in a situation of conflict then you should postpone any new endeavour.

Line 2: *Humility has become recognized. With firm correctness there will be good fortune.*

Only those who are valued for their modesty of character are entrusted with important tasks. Your inner self is shown by your outward conduct and behaviour, which is noted by others and judged accordingly.

Line 3: *The wise man of acknowledged merit will maintain his success to the end, and have good fortune.*

If you are successful you will attract attention. Do not allow this to turn your head and lead you into conceit and immodesty. If you retain modesty you will retain the loving regard and supportive friendship of others.

Line 4: *One whose action would in every way be advantageous, increases the more his humility.*

Don't shirk the work and responsibilities which are given to you, or look for the means of doing nothing with your time and energy. Others depend on you and you are responsible to them.

Line 5: *One, without being rich, is able to employ his neighbours. He may advantageously use the force of arms. All his movements will be advantageous.*

Modesty does not mean being ineffectual. Sometimes you have to be authoritative to get things done. But you must retain clarity and tact. You may be given responsibility for completing a task. It would be modest and wise to ask for guidance from another.

Line 6: *Humility that has made itself recognized. The humble man will with advantage put his troops in motion; but he will only punish his own towns and state.*

If you fall into immodesty then you will come into conflict

with others, even those you are in close harmony with. You must look to yourself and correct your faults. Restore your harmonious relations with others by returning to the path of modesty and humility.

Hexagram 16
Yu—Enthusiasm

Component Trigrams

Primary: Chen—Thunder (upper), K'un—Earth (lower). Nuclear: K'an—Water (above), Ken—The Mountain (below).

Keywords

Thunder, earth, groups, harmony, joy, opportunity, caution, preparation.

Commentary

Some goal you have long planned for is now within reach. You must act boldly now if you want to achieve it. Involving those you have authority over in a well-devised and sound plan will increase your probability of success. Make sure, though, that you have left nothing to chance otherwise the consequences could be costly for you. If you take the correct action now with all the enthusiasm you can muster then you cannot fail and will be well rewarded.

Judgement.

It is to one's advantage to set up princes as allies, and to put the army in motion.

Your enthusiasm will inspire those around you to combine with you in a joint endeavour which will achieve great success.

Interpretation

In the upper position of the hexagram is thunder and movement, in the lower is earth and obedience. These ideas combined give the concept of enthusiasm. The yang fourth line is regarded as the principal administrator of the ruler. With thunder comes movement and the earth obeys. Enthusiasm for action from within you, arouses and attracts the enthusiasm of others.

Image

Thunder issuing from the earth with a crashing noise. The ancient kings composed their music and did honour to virtue, presenting it especially and most grandly to God, when they associated with Him at the service, their highest ancestor and their father.

Dwelling on the power and mystery of the spiritual brings harmony and happiness.

Line readings

Line 1: *One proclaims one's pleasure and satisfaction. There will be misfortune.*

If you are boastful or overbearing then people will distance themselves from you.

Line 2: *One is as firm as a rock. One sees a thing without waiting till it has come to pass. With firm correctness there will be good fortune.*

Make sure your enthusiasm doesn't carry you or others away; temper it with common sense and your sense of responsibility to yourself and others.

Line 3: *One looks upwards for favours while indulging the feeling of pleasure and satisfaction. If one does change there will be occasion for repentance.*

Act out of your own sense of judgement and your enthusiastic desire for getting something done now. Don't allow yourself to be swayed or led astray by those above you who you find glamorous or exciting. Have faith in yourself and your own judgement.

Line 4: *He who brings harmony and satisfaction. Great is the success which he obtains. Let him not allow suspicions to enter his mind, and thus friends will gather around him.*

Others admire and respect your honesty and sincerity of commitment. Your support of them will be reciprocated.

Line 5: *He has a chronic complaint, but lives on without dying.*

Feeling under pressure, although onerous and disliked, is sometimes the impetus you need to take appropriate and effective action.

Line 6: *One with darkened mind is devoted to the pleasure and satisfaction of the time; but if he change his course even when it may be considered as completed, there will be no error.*

You have been carried away by your enthusiasm and your delight in yourself. It is necessary to come back down to earth and view yourself and your circumstances objectively. This clarity of perception can only be of benefit to you in the future.

Hexagram 17
Sui—Following

Component Trigrams

Primary: Tui—Marsh (upper), Chen—Thunder (lower). Nuclear: Sun—Wind (above), Ken—The Mountain (below).

Keywords

Marsh, thunder, listening, following, cooperation, opportunity, counsel.

Commentary

Let others take the initiative just now. Follow their guidance and advice about the direction you should take and the goal you should aim for and your undertaking will be a success, with great benefits for you. If you rashly go your own way and ignore good advice then you put yourself at risk of failure and subsequent remorse. Those who you assume to be in opposition to you could in fact be willing and ready to help you. If you successfully obtain the help of others then you will be closer to obtaining a great reward.

Judgement

There will be great progress and success. But it will be advantageous to be firm and correct. There will then be no error.

Those who lead must be worthy of the faith and trust that others put in them. If they are not, the result will be failure for all.

Interpretation

In the hexagram's structure the arousing (thunder) humbles itself beneath delight (the lowly marsh). The upper trigram also signifies the eldest son and the lower signifies the youngest daughter. These suggestions combine to yield the ideas of following and follower. Knowing when to follow rather than lead is a wise attribute. Happiness creates harmony. If you are happy and content and have faith and trust in those around you then no harm can come from following them. Also, the one who is being followed must show in his character and actions that he is worthy of the support that he receives.

Image

Thunder hidden in the midst of the marsh. The wise man, when it is getting towards dark, enters his house and rests.

As situations change, so should you; but stay true to yourself. Being flexible and adaptable is more realistic and sensible than stubbornly trying to resist change.

Line readings

Line 1: *One changes the object of one's pursuit; but if one is firm and correct, there will be good fortune. Going beyond one's own gate to find associates, one will achieve merit.*

Open your self and your mind up to the views and attitudes of others. Be prepared to abandon your ideas for new ones suggested by others. Widen the circle of people that you listen and relate to, even at the risk of possible conflict.

Line 2: *One cleaves to the little boy, and lets go the man of age and experience.*

You must be wary of becoming involved with those who are not honest and sincere. They will ensnare you in their weakness. Distance yourself from them.

Line 3: *One cleaves to the man of age and experience, and lets go the little boy. Such following will get what it seeks; but it will be advantageous to adhere to what is firm and correct.*

You must decide for yourself the direction that will also allow you to keep faith with yourself. Then bond yourself with those who share common cause with you.

Line 4: *One is followed and obtains adherence. Though one is firm and correct, there will be misfortune. If one is sincere however in one's course, and makes that evident, into what error will one fall?*

When you are in a position of authority don't be swayed or misled by the insincere praise of those who wish to gain influence with you. Make your decisions from your own honest judgement, remembering your responsibility to yourself and others, and then make them clear to those around you.

Line 5: *The ruler is sincere in fostering all that is excellent. There will be good fortune.*

Be guided by the powers of virtue and truth in the path you chose. Stay true to yourself and you will succeed.

Line 6: *Sincerity firmly held and clung to, and bound fast. With it, the king presents his offerings on the western mountain.*

Ask a more experienced and wiser person than yourself to give you help and advice in your undertaking. It will be of benefit to you both.

Hexagram 18
Ku—Work on disruption

Component Trigrams

Primary: Ken—The Mountain (upper), Sun—Wind (lower). Nuclear: Chen—Thunder (above), Tui—Marsh (below).

Keywords

The mountain, wind, corruption, disorder, illicitness, sickness, past errors, reconciliation.

Commentary

You find yourself in an unusually difficult and confused situation, but one which also presents you with a great opportunity. There is a deep-rooted disorder in your circumstances, perhaps in your self and your relationships. The possibility is there, though, of restoring this situation to one of health and harmony. It will require much of you: in terms of strength of mind and character, your sincerity and good faith, and prolonged effort. You will have to discover the root causes of the problem and remedy them accordingly. When things are restored to wholeness, you will receive great benefits.

Judgement

There will be great progress and success. There will be advantage in crossing the great stream. One should weigh well the events of three days before the turning point, and those to be done three days after it.

You must apply yourself with strength and energy to finding the origins of the present decay and disorder, in order to bring it to and end and restore the situation to well-being.

Interpretation

This hexagram expresses a state of decay. The mountain blocks the wind. Stagnant air is redolent with corruption. But the hexagram also presents a reversal of this. A restoration of wholeness that will be the precursor to eventual success. This will only be achieved by great effort though. There is festering corruption around you which has been bred by dishonesty and deceit. You must counter this by bringing the qualities of clear-sightedness, honesty and sincerity to bear on it.

Image

The wind blows low on the mountain. The wise man addresses himself to help the people and nourish his own virtue.

This image embodies the message of the hexagram's component trigrams. It emphasizes how others can help if given the right lead: making clear what is required and being honest and sincere.

Line readings

Line 1: *A son deals with the troubles caused by his father. If he be an able son, the father will escape the blame of having erred. The position is perilous, but there will be good fortune in the end.*

To get to the bottom of this situation and change it, it will be necessary for you to re-examine the basis on which you act and form relationships, your guiding principles, and reform them if necessary. But be very cautious as this will have lasting and far-reaching consequences.

Line 2: *A son deals with the troubles caused by his mother. He should not carry his firm correctness to the utmost.*

Patience and sensitivity to others, the use of tact and diplomacy: these must be the means to making the changes that are required.

Line 3: *A son deals with the troubles caused by his father. There may be small occasion for repentance, but there will not be any great error.*

You must commit yourself to making the necessary changes

with wholehearted effort and energy. This will bring about resentment from others but you must persist, all the same.

Line 4: *A son views indulgently the troubles caused by his father. If he go forward, he will find cause to regret it.*

There is no time to waste, you must act now to transform the corrupt situation and you must keep up your efforts no matter what setbacks you face along the way. Be vigilant over any tendency in yourself to turn away or slacken off.

Line 5: *A son deals with the troubles caused by his father. He obtains the praise of using the fit instrument for his work.*

Others will applaud your honesty and courage in acknowledging your responsibility for things being as bad as they are and your determined efforts to change yourself and transform the situation. They may be inspired to join you and work with you.

Line 6: *One does not serve either king or prince, but in a lofty spirit prefers to attend to one's own affairs.*

You responsibility is to the future, to the effort and selfless concern needed to create a fresh, new beginning. Don't concern yourself with what is past and troublesome. Dwell instead on happy things with their invigorating and restorative value. In this spirit focus on yourself and your motivating principles. Work toward change for yourself and others.

Hexagram 19
Lin—Advance

Component Trigrams

Primary: K'un—Earth (upper), Tui—Marsh (lower). Nuclear: K'un—Earth (above), Chen—Thunder (below).

Keywords

Earth, marsh, ascent, increasing power, moral strength, generosity, benevolence.

Commentary

You are in a very auspicious situation. What you are about to undertake will be highly effective and successful. There will be no need for force. What will be required is proper conduct and a sense of caution. You are in an impressively favourable situation but remember that it won't last. Beware of letting your good fortune go to your head. Keep in mind that things change; maintain honesty and sincerity. Share your good fortune with others. While your star remains in the ascendancy, and you continue to act properly, you can enjoy your success.

Judgement

There will be great progress and success, while it will be advantageous to be firmly correct. In the eighth month there will be evil.

Spring brings new growth and gladness. But as the seasons change, so do all situations. Therefore, all you should do now is continue to ensure the worth of your principles and conduct.

Interpretation

The hexagram has two strong yang lines advancing on four yielding yin lines, which gives an image of the advent of expanding power and authority. This is a hexagram of growth and strength. You are required to remain steadfast to true aims and motives in the midst of favourable, but ephemeral, time. The undertaking you are about to begin will have great power and impact and will be a success. Don't be impetuous and forceful. All you need do is proceed with due care, and with regard for good conduct and respect toward others, and success is inevitable.

Image

The waters of a marsh and the earth above it. The wise man has his purposes of instruction that are inexhaustible, and nourishes and supports the people without limit.

Change is infinite and eternal. So is learning and knowledge. The wise man knows this and will seek to teach others.

Line readings

Line 1: *One advances in company. Through firm correctness there will be good fortune.*

You are being effortlessly carried forward by favourable circumstances. Don't lose your head.

Line 2: *One advances in company. There will be good fortune; advancing will be in every way advantageous.*

You cannot neglect your spiritual nature while you are enjoying worldly success, as nothing on earth endures.

Line 3: *One is well-pleased to advance, but one's action will be in no way advantageous. If one becomes anxious about it however, there will be no error.*

Don't get arrogant or complacent. Think of others and be generous to them. Correct any faults in yourself and your conduct.

Line 4: *One advances in the highest mode. There will be no error.*

New people may now come into your life; you should welcome them and be open and supportive.

Line 5: *The advance of wisdom, such as befits the great ruler. There will be good fortune.*

Choose carefully who will help you and the tasks that you give them. Trust them to fulfil their allotted tasks successfully, as they trust you to fulfil yours.

Line 6: *The advance of honesty and generosity. There will be good fortune and no error.*

From the solitary, spiritual region of your joy and success, it is now time to return to the world and share with others what you have learned.

Hexagram 20
Kuan—Contemplating

Component Trigrams

Primary: Sun—Wind (upper), K'un—Earth (lower). Nuclear: Ken—The Mountain (above), K'un—Earth (below).

Keywords

Wind, earth, manifestation, showing, watching, perception, observance.

Commentary

Look, listen and learn: these are the keywords. It would be better, more prudent, to stay in your present situation and scrutinize it carefully than attempt to move forward into new and unknown territory. There may soon be a change for the worse in your circumstances. Study closely the direction and aims, the motives and conduct of yourself and those you are closely associated with. Be prepared to accept just criticism and advice. Only when you have thoroughly assessed, in a clear and objective light, your present situation will you then be able to consider moving forward. Through this process of review you may discover an important matter, with close relevance to you and your situation. Deal with it carefully and thoughtfully and you will then be better equipped to continue on your course.

Judgement

The worshipper has washed his hands but has not yet presented his offerings. His sincerity and dignity commands a reverent regard.

Everything is able to be seen: past, present and future.

Interpretation

In the hexagram the four weak yin lines look up reverently to the two strong yang lines. This symbolizes the strength and authority of the wise man manifesting itself to others he can show and teach. A great wind (the upper trigram) blows across the earth (the lower trigram). It would be better to survey the landscape before venturing forward into such a wind. This refers to the idea of contemplating the present situation. Cultivate clear-sightedness and the proper way. Be an example that others can recognize and follow.

Image

The wind moves across the earth. The ancient kings examined the different regions of the kingdom, to see the ways of the people, and set forth their instructions.

The ruler comes among the people to observe and teach. His gratified people show their respect and loyalty.

Line readings

Line 1: *A thoughtless boy; not blameable in men of inferior rank, but matter for regret in wise man.*

Don't just look at the superficial, the fanciful and sensational. To grow in wisdom you must grow in your understanding of others. Look more deeply at others in order to understand their actions and their motives.

Line 2: *One peeps out from a door. It would be advantageous if it were merely the firm correctness of a female.*

Only if you take a wider view of things will you be able to see them clearly and put them into a proper perspective.

Line 3: *One looks at the course of one's life, to advance or recede accordingly.*

You must try to see yourself as others see you. Examine yourself thoroughly before deciding which direction you should take.

Line 4: *One contemplating the glory of the kingdom. It will be advantageous for him, being such as he is, to seek to be guest of the king.*

Having learned from the past you should seek positions of responsibility and authority.

Line 5: *One contemplates one's own life-course. A wise man will thus fall into no error.*

To be worthy of others' respect you should conscientiously survey all aspects of yourself. But remember that the point of this introspection is to make self-judgements and then act on those judgements.

Line 6: *One contemplates one's character to see if it be indeed that of a wise man. One will not fall into error.*

At this stage you have completed you period of inner contemplation. Although you are moving on, purged of your past faults and weakness, don't forget the past: otherwise you will repeat the mistakes of the past in the future.

Hexagram 21
Shih Ho—Biting through

Component Trigrams

Primary: Li—Fire (upper), Chen—Thunder (lower). Nuclear: K'an—Water (above), Ken—The Mountain (below).

Keywords

Thunder, lightning, clarity, shining brilliance, justice, attachment, clinging, union.

Commentary

You must not flinch from your purpose despite the obstacles you face. Rely on the rightness of your cause and maintain your commitment and you will win through. Remain in harmony with those above and below you. Working in tandem with others to achieve your goal will allow you to robustly defend your worthy course. Don't forsake your basic principles and your forceful action will be successful. Prepare, though, to cope with conflict on the way.

Judgement

There will be successful progress. It will be advantageous to use legal restraints.

You have to act now to remove obstacles from your path, but you must not do this by unworthy conduct.

Interpretation

The name of the hexagram derives from its shape: the top and bottom yang lines are the lips, the yin lines are teeth and the fourth yang line is something being bitten through. High and low must unite: what separates the two jaws must be bitten through. The trigram images of thunder and fire symbolize the rule of law. You may need to employ some kind of force to reach your goal. The hexagram is to do with biting past obstacles, eliminating problems and disunion, curbing spiteful threats and sorting out legal difficulties.

Image

Thunder and lightning. The ancient kings framed their penalties with intelligence, and promulgated their laws.

A just, open and clear set of rules, with clearly identified penalties for transgressions, is necessary to deal with those who don't follow the right conduct.

Line readings

Line 1: *One with his feet in the stocks and deprived of his toes. There will be no error.*

First offences should be treated less severely than further transgressions. Having erred, though, there is still scope for remorse and atonement. Return to the right path and there will be no lasting harm.

Line 2: *Biting through the soft flesh, and going on to bite off the nose. There will be no error.*

In response to provocation you are meting out penalties which are too severe. Perhaps you are justified.

Line 3: *One gnaws dried flesh, and meets with what is disagreeable. There will be occasion for some small regret, but no great error.*

Don't concern yourself with issues that are dead and buried.

Line 4: *One gnaws the flesh dried on the bone, and gets pledges of money and arrows. It will be advantageous to him to realize the difficulty of the his task and be firm, in which case there will be good fortune.*

Your obstacles and enemies are strong; you must be stronger and harder. Be firm and unwavering and you will win through.

Line 5: *One gnaws at dried flesh, and finds the yellow gold. Let him be firm and correct, realizing the peril of his position. There will be no error.*

What you have to do may be clear and simple but don't relax your attitude of rigorous purpose. Be steadfast and don't retreat before vigorous opposition.

Line 6: *One is wearing the wooden yoke and is deprived of his ears. There will be misfortune.*

The transgressor, and that may be yourself, is arrogant, stubborn and shameless. These faults and weaknesses must be tackled and remedied.

Hexagram 22
Pi—Adornment

Component Trigrams

Primary: Ken—The Mountain (upper), Li—Fire (lower). Nuclear: Chen—Thunder (above), K'an—Water (lower).

Keywords

Mountain, fire, grace, beauty, sunsets, coherence, the arts.

Commentary

Your present situation is settled but as you go forward you will encounter surprises. It is wiser to not to be too ambitious and to restrict yourself to what you can cope with. Put your efforts and energy into maintaining proper conduct and a harmonious balance between yourself and your environment, and between yourself and others.

Judgement

There should be free course. There will be little advance, however, if it be allowed to advance and take the lead.

Concern with adornment must not become excessive or obsessive; there are other matters to attend to. The quality of just and elegant rules depends on the merit of those who administer them.

Interpretation

The hexagram combines clarity (lower trigram) with the unmoving (upper). At night the fire illuminates the mountain. This introduces the symbol of adornment and beauty. The hexagram is about elegance and brightness. Its concern is with artistic and theoretical activities rather than prosaic, everyday ones. It intimates that one should simply occupy oneself with artistic adornment while remaining true and humble. But if required one should relinquish this in the face of trouble. Grace and elegance, nevertheless, are worthy of attainment. This hexagram is about the value of beauty and harmony and those who create and admire these qualities. It also refers to the impression we make on others and how this accords with our view of ourselves.

Image

Fire illuminates the mountain. The wise man throws a brilliancy around his various processes of government, but does not dare in a similar way to decide cases of criminal litigation.

Meditation brings peace but it does not remove the necessity for choice and action.

Line readings

Line 1: *One adorns the way of his feet. One can discard a carriage and walk on foot.*

Don't always take the easy option. People will respect you for taking on what is difficult.

Line 2: *One adorns one's beard.*

Trying simply to please other people has an adverse effect on your character.

Line 3: *One is adorned and bedewed with rich favours. But maintain firm correctness, and there will be good fortune.*

Don't let yourself be corrupted by love of the good things in life.

Line 4: *One is adorned, but only in white. As if mounted on a white horse, and furnished with wings, he seeks union, while another pursues, not as a robber, but intent on a matrimonial alliance.*

Don't neglect your true path and friends in order to impress the wider world.

Line 5: *One is adorned by the occupants of the heights and gardens. He bears his roll of silk, small and slight. He may appear stingy; but there will be good fortune in the end.*

Bonding with a soul mate after the glitter of the superficial world will at first make you feel humble and unworthy. But this sincere friendship will be valuable.

Line 6: *One's only ornament is white. There will be no error.*

Some happy people have simple grace from within and have no need of the external trappings of beauty.

Hexagram 23
Po—Splitting apart

Component Trigrams

Primary: Ken—The Mountain (upper), K'un—Earth (lower).
Nuclear: K'un—Earth (above), K'un—Earth (below).

Keywords

Mountain, earth, division, disintegration, challenge, contemplation, endurance.

Commentary

This inauspicious situation should be viewed as a salutary reminder of the fickleness of fortune and of the need to be adaptable to changing circumstances. You are threatened by subversive forces but if you maintain strength of character and use your faculties of wise discernment and judgement, then you will be able to decide on the best courses of action. You must unflinchingly commit yourself to a preparatory period of self-examination. Although you may suffer a setback you will come back from it stronger for the experience.

Judgement

It will not be advantageous to make a movement in any direction whatever.

It is better to stay in the background when the worst 'are full of a passionate conviction' and making all the running.

Interpretation

The solid top yang line seems about to give way to the division below it. The mountain sits uneasily on the unreliable earth. The hexagram deals with how one survives in threatening and destructive circumstances. It reminds of the fickleness of fate and the necessity of having the correct resources to deal with adversity. The situation is unbalanced and lacks harmony. You should refrain from action until the position improves.

Image

The mountain adheres to the earth. Superiors seek to strengthen those below them, to secure the peace and stability of their own position.

Authority and respect, love and loyalty can only be attained and survive by generosity towards others.

Line readings

Line 1: *One overturns the couch by injuring its legs. The injury will go on to the destruction of all firm correctness, and there will be misfortune.*

Others are trying to subvert your position but if you act now you will fail. Wait.

Line 2: *One overthrows the couch by injuring its frame. The injury will go on to the destruction of all firm correctness, and there will be misfortune.*

You feel isolated and helpless and are responding prematurely to the subverting challenge. Be careful, as this will result in failure.

Line 3: *One is among the overthrowers; but there will be no error.*

Because of your isolation you decide to make an accommodation with those who threaten you and call a truce. This is forgivable.

Line 4: *One has overthrown the couch, and is going to injure he who lies on it. There will be misfortune.*

A line of abject failure and total defeat. It is your fate and you must endure it.

Line 5: *One leads on the others like a string of fishes, and obtains for them the favour that lights on the inmates of the palace. There will be advantage in every way.*

You recover and take action, which improves your situation financially and in other ways. You may be helped by someone.

Line 6: *A great fruit has not been eaten. The wise man finds the people again as a chariot carrying him. The small men by their course overthrow their own dwellings.*

You have suffered and endured but things are not the same nor as good as they were before. All you can do is accept it and start anew from where you are. It is pointless and useless to dwell on the past and what has been lost. Be optimistic and look to the future. Others will come to your aid at this time of need.

Hexagram 24
Fu—Returning

Component Trigrams

Primary: K'un—Earth (upper), Chen—Thunder (lower). Nuclear: K'un—Earth (above), K'un—Earth (below).

Keywords

Thunder, earth, turning point, approaching spring, ascent, gradual, improvement, reinforcement.

Commentary

This is a time of growing good fortune and especially favourable for any new undertaking. Be cautious though, don't get too far ahead of the awakening forces that will support you. Conserve your energies and concentrate on keeping to your true path and character. Your time is arriving and you will undoubtedly benefit.

Judgement

There will be free course and progress. One finds no-one to distress one in one's exits and entrances; friends come to one and no error is committed. One will return and repeat one's proper course; in seven days comes return. There will be advantage in whatever direction movement is made.

As you wait for the full effects of this time of beneficial change to emerge, you should think carefully and plan for the future.

Interpretation

The trigram positions show thunder within the earth, representing the first tremors of great force. The hexagram describes the unending, cyclic movements of decay and renewal. This is an auspicious hexagram, marking the beginning of a period of recovery after reaching the nadir of decline. As the seasons change and winter begins the long preparation for spring, so your fortunes will change for the better.

Image

Thunder silent in the midst of the earth. The ancient kings on the day of the winter solstice, shut the gates of the passes from one state to another, so that the travelling merchants could not then pursue their journeys, nor the princes go on with the inspection of their states.

Winter was a time of rest and recuperation, a withdrawing inwards to aid the renewal of energy.

Line readings

Line 1: *One returns from an error of no great extent, which will not proceed to anything requiring repentance. There will be great good fortune.*

Don't stray off your own true path or you may end up doing something you will later regret.

Line 2: *An admired return. There will be good fortune.*

Encouraged by being surrounded by influential people, you sense a new beginning. You are considering an offer of help you have received.

Line 3: *One has made repeated returns. The position is perilous, but there will be no error.*

Remember: 'The only thing we have to fear, is fear itself.' Don't be afraid to grasp your new opportunities. Change is inevitable and you should eagerly welcome it when it brings you good fortune. Your stop-go attitude is wasteful and self-defeating. You must go forward optimistically without stopping or turning back.

Line 4: *One moves in the centre among others, and yet returns alone to one's proper path.*

You have to go your own way even at the risk of offending others. Don't feel bad about that. A respected person will give you help.

Line 5: *One makes a noble return. There will be no ground for repentance.*

You have to accept and go along with change and others around you will eventually realize this. Your exemplary attitude and behaviour may encourage them to follow you.

Line 6: *One is all astray on the subject of returning. There will be misfortune. There will be calamities and errors. If with his views he puts the troops in motion, the end will be a great defeat, whose issues will extend to the ruler of the state. Even in ten years he will not be able to repair the disaster.*

Afraid of forsaking the old and familiar you have let the opportunity of change for the better pass you by. This is a profound error which may have lasting detrimental consequences for you. This was your decisive moment; you may never have another. You have rejected a rare opportunity and all you can do now is wait for a lesser opportunity to come round.

Hexagram 25
Wu Wang—Correctness

Component Trigrams
Primary: Ch'ien—Heaven (upper), Li—Thunder (lower). Nuclear: Sun—Wind (above), Ken—The Mountain (below).

Keywords
Heaven, thunder, beginnings, passivity, naturalness, innocence, guilelessness, sincerity.

Commentary
If you act rashly or selfishly in your present situation you will be afflicted with unusually severe ill-luck. Be modest, sincere and

honest with others. Don't try to force your own way just now. Be content to go along with things as they unfold naturally and you will be fine. Take great care not to act impetuously or in a domineering way for selfish ends. If your motives and acts are impure you will face great misfortune.

Judgement

There will be great progress and success. It will be advantageous to be firm and correct. If one is not correct, one will fall into errors, and it will not be advantageous to move in any direction.

By following the way of heaven in all innocence one is as one should be. Failure awaits lack of innocence.

Interpretation

Beneath heaven, thunder sounds; elemental energy which is innocent. Those who act out of innocent selflessness: good fortune. For those who conspire for their own selfish gain: evil fortune. The hexagram signifies being in tune with one's true nature and the way of heaven. This is the state of harmony and innocence.

Image

The thunder rolls under heaven, and to everything there is given its nature, free from all insincerity. The ancient kings made their regulations in complete accordance with the seasons, thereby nourishing all things.

Thunder brings rain which nourishes the germination and growth of plants. It is wise to act in harmony with natural forces.

Line readings

Line 1: *One is free from all insincerity. One's advance will be accompanied with good fortune.*

Trust your intuition and you will have good fortune.

Line 2: *One reaps without having ploughed, and gathers the produce of his third year's fields without having cultivated them the first year for that end. To such a one there will be advantage in whatever direction he may move.*

Don't try to achieve everything by one action now; you will fail. But if your action is for short-term aims then it is fine.

Line 3: *Calamity happens to one who is free from insincerity, as in the case of an ox that has been tied up. A passerby finds it and*

*carries it off, while the people in the neighbourhood have the ca-
lamity of being accused and apprehended.*

Be stoic and fatalistic about the ill-fortune that surrounds you.
Your loss is another's gain.

Line 4: *If one remains firm and correct, there will be no error.*

Keep to the path you know is yours and don't be influenced by
others.

Line 5: *One is free from insincerity, and yet has fallen ill. Not using medicine, one will have occasion for joy in one's recovery.*

The ill-fortune that dogs you will end and, in time, you will recover. Being anxious will only make your position worse.

Line 6: *One is free from insincerity, yet sure to fall into error, if one
take action. One's action will not be advantageous in any way.*

Refrain from all action, even that prompted by intuition, and
wait patiently.

Hexagram 26
Tach'u—Taming force

Component Trigrams

Primary: Ken—The Mountain (upper), Ch'ien—Heaven (lower).
Nuclear: Chen—Thunder (above), Tui—Marsh (below).

Keywords

The mountain, heaven, stillness, creativity, restraint, accumulation, virtue.

Commentary

Cultivate your talents and strive to be of good character and conduct. You will be able to tackle even formidably difficult undertakings and be sure of help from influential others and success.
You show your worthiness by accumulating these heavenly creative energies within. To use them for some common good would
be an even worthier act, and you should consider this. Use what
you glean from the experience and example of others and you
will overcome immediate obstacles and find lasting success.

Judgement

It will be advantageous to be firm and correct. If one does not seek to enjoy one's revenues in one's own family, without taking service at court, there will be good fortune. It will be advantageous to cross the great stream.

The wise man partakes of periods of stillness and quiet each day to strengthen his character. Any activity to do with the public good is favourable.

Interpretation

Heaven resides within the mountain; great potential is stored up. The hexagram conveys the idea of containment and restraint, and this causing great forces to build up. There is great potential within you which you should use wisely. This hexagram signifies the balance of inner strength with outward calmness. It is about containment and restraint, steadfastness and strength of purpose.

Image

Heaven within the mountain. The wise man stores largely in his memory the words and deeds of former men, to subserve the accumulation of his virtue.

Learning from past errors and past successes ensure future success.

Line readings

Line 1: *One is in a position of peril. It will be advantageous to stop advancing.*

Forging forward at this time will only produce error and failure. Wait patiently.

Line 2: *A carriage has its braking strap removed from underneath.*

If you find yourself in a weak position the pragmatic and sensible thing is to do nothing and wait.

Line 3: *One urges his way with good horses. It will be advantageous for him to realize the difficulty of his course, and to be firm and correct, exercising himself daily in his charioteering and methods of defence; then there will be advantage in whatever direction he may advance.*

Well-prepared for the problems you will face ahead, you can go forward towards your goal with confidence.

Line 4: *A young bull has a piece of wood over his horns. There will be great good fortune.*

Immediate action will neutralize any potential harm.

Line 5: *The tusk of a gelded hog. There will be good fortune.*

Action now to affect the nature of your potential enemies will diminish the threat they pose to you.

Line 6: *One is in command of the firmament of heaven. There will be progress.*

Everything has been favourable and you have achieved your goals.

Hexagram 27
I—Nourishment

Component Trigrams

Primary: Ken—The Mountain (upper), Chen—Thunder (lower).
Nuclear: K'un—Earth (above), K'un—Earth (lower).

Keywords

The mountain, thunder, temperance, self-discipline, discretion, opportunity.

Commentary

This is an auspicious time. You have to chose what is to be nourished —in yourself or in another—after proper and worthy deliberation. The path to this choice being true you will achieve particular success. This is a remarkable opportunity and if you chose that aspect of your own nature or another's that most deserves this enrichment then you will benefit from good fortune. However, if you merely satisfy the cruder appetites you will come to regret it.

Judgement

With firm correctness there will be good fortune. We must look at what we are seeking to nourish, and by the exercise of out thoughts seek for the proper sustenance.

Be sensible and careful about your material and other nourishment. Look after yourself and others who require it.

Interpretation

Thunder at the base of the mountain; movement below stillness: the first stirrings of life activity. Taken together with the visual symbolism of a mouth in the hexagram, this suggest the idea of nourishment: physical, mental and spiritual. Be careful what you consume in terms of food and drink as it may not be nourishing, just as you may be wrong about your own nature. Think of your spiritual needs.

Image

Thunder within the mountain. The wise man enjoins watchfulness over our words, and the temperate regulation of our eating and drinking.

Being temperate and thoughtful in what you say and in the nourishment you take, and your consideration for yourself and others, will bring you to wisdom.

Line readings

Line 1: *One leaves his efficacious tortoise, and looks at the other till his jaw hangs down.*

You render yourself unworthy and obnoxious with base envy and greed

Line 2: *One looks downward for nourishment, which is contrary to what is proper; or seeking it from the height above, advance towards which will lead to misfortune.*

You must look first of all to yourself for nourishment and succour. To lazily seek others to provide it is bad.

Line 3: *One acts contrary to the method of nourishing. However firm he may be, there will be misfortune. For ten years let him not take any action, for it will not be in any way advantageous.*

You are lost in the worthless pursuit of sensational pleasure.

Line 4: *One looks downwards for the power to nourish. There will be good fortune. Looking with a tiger's downward unwavering glare, and with his desire that impels him to spring after spring, one will fall into no error.*

You know that you need and must enlist the support of others to achieve your aims. Seize any opportunity that comes your way.

Line 5: *One acts contrary to what is regular and proper; but if one abides in firmness, there will be good fortune. One should not, however, try to cross the great stream.*

Don't take on too much. Know your limitations and seek appropriate help.

Line 6: *He who brings the nourishing. His position is perilous, but there will be good fortune. It will be advantageous to cross the great stream.*

You are fortunate. Your nourishing spiritual nature can be used for the good of others What you undertake for the benefit of others will be successful.

Hexagram 28
Ta Kuo—Exceeding greatness

Component Trigrams

Primary: Tui—Marsh (upper), Sun—Wind (lower). Nuclear: Ch'ien—Heaven (above), Ch'ien—Heaven (below).

Keywords

Marsh, tree, heaviness, flexibility, caution, great developments, renunciation, solitude, continuation.

Commentary

You are in a particularly critical situation but if you have the right and proper attitude you can expect things to favour your winning through. Act boldly and confidently and this unusually threatening situation may be completely defused. Assessing how you should go about this undertaking is an important prior step, taking your own nature and all other circumstances into consideration. Then take the action you consider the most appropriate and you will be successful. The needs of the situation should decide your actions, not your inflexible inclinations.

Judgement

The beam is weak. There will be advantage in moving in any direction whatever; there will be success.

It is necessary to find some means to redress the imbalance, as there is not enough strength.

Interpretation

The Sun trigram here represents a solitary tree with the water risen above it, symbolizing solitude and renunciation. This is the recommended course during times of severe trouble and conflict. The hexagram has two weak outer lines and four strong inner lines, and resembles a roof with a strong centre but weak edges. The centre is in danger of falling. The hexagram signifies caution and the need for change.

Image

Trees hidden beneath the waters of the marsh. The wise man stands alone, has no fear, and keeps retired from the world without regret.

   Isolation may be necessary to survive this testing time.

Line readings

Line 1: *One spreads rush-mats under things set on the ground. There will be no error.*

   Be cautious and take precautions, and ignore others' comments. Provide a firm basis for any new venture.

Line 2: *A decayed willow produces shoots, an old husband with a young wife. There will be advantage in every way.*

   The outlook is providential for a new undertaking, new love, new spirituality.

Line 3: *A beam is weak. There will be misfortune.*

   You have ignored warning-signs and taken no precautions. It would be too dangerous to do anything for the time being.

Line 4: *A beam curves upwards. There will be good fortune. If one looks for other help there will be cause for regret.*

   Welcome help has come from another but don't exploit this person for your own ends otherwise you will regret it.

Line 5: *A decayed willow produces flowers, an old wife with a young husband. There will be occasion neither for blame nor for praise.*

   Don't arrogantly forsake old friendships when you are successful. They are still part of your destiny as you have not changed as much as you think.

Line 6: *One wades with extraordinary boldness through a stream, till the water hides the crown of his head. There will be misfortune, but no ground for blame.*

Through lack of caution and foresight, your own enthusiasm and commitment has brought you into hard times. But you can learn from what is only a temporary setback.

Hexagram 29
K'an—The deep

Component Trigrams

Primary: K'an—Water (upper), K'an—Water (lower). Nuclear: Ken—The Mountain (above), Chen—Thunder (below).

Keywords

Water, danger, decline, lack of bearings, caution.

Commentary

You are in a position of danger. The best way to overcome this is to move boldly and remain true to yourself. You must assess your situation carefully and though the choices open to you at the moment are unappealing, with patience and clearsightedness you should arrive at a better situation. You may be faced with great challenges and fearful situations, but if you maintain strength of heart and remain true you will survive, having learned valuable things.

Judgement

When one is sincere, the mind is penetrating. Actions will be of high value. Remain steadfast in the face of danger, and true to yourself. Keep going forward, as any hesitation could be disastrous.

Interpretation

This hexagram concerns danger. The trigrams are water upon water, and suggest not only dangerous waters but also perilous pits, hazardous caves and other similar situations. The hexagram is about how to meet danger, what effects it can have on you, and how to escape and survive it.

Image

Water flowing continuously on. The wise man maintains constantly the virtue of his heart and the integrity of his conduct, and practices the business of instruction.

If you remain virtuous then you will not be swamped by danger.

Line readings

Line 1: *One is in the double defile, and yet enters a cavern within it. There will be misfortune.*

Do not make the mistake of becoming casual about danger if it is always around you. Remain vigilant.

Line 2: *One is in all the peril of the defile. One will, however, get a little of the deliverance that one seeks.*

Focus on achieving limited aims rather than going all out.

Line 3: *One is confronted by a defile, whether one comes or goes. All is peril and unrest. One's endeavours will lead into the cavern of the pit. There should be no action in such a case.*

When you seem to be in a 'no-win' situation it is time to halt temporarily to think your way out. Continuing to act is foolish.

Line 4: *One is at a feast with a simple bottle of spirits and a basket of rice, while the cups and bowls are only of earthenware. One introduces important lessons as the ruler's intelligence admits. There will in the end be no error.*

You must cut you losses and settle for less and accept help from areas you would have previously scorned. Be grateful to those who help and accept the help in the sincere and honest spirit in which it is given.

Line 5: *The defile is almost full of water; but order will soon be brought about. There will be no error.*

There is still danger around so don't embark on anything new. Keep everything simple.

Line 6: *One is bound with cords and placed in the thicket of thorns. But in three years he does not learn the course for him to pursue. There will be misfortune.*

Everything has come down upon your head at once. You have brought this upon yourself. You have to carefully trace the relation between your motives and this calamitous outcome. Examine your character and remedy whatever is at fault.

Hexagram 30
Li—Fire

Component Trigrams

Primary: Li—Fire (upper), Li—Fire (lower). Nuclear: Tui—Marsh (above), Sun—Wind (below).

Keywords

Beauty, sunlight, shining brilliance, intelligence, clinging.

Commentary

You have an opportunity to be creative. Stay on a true path, be humble and listen to advice from experienced others. Give careful though to the advice before accepting or rejecting it. Your collaboration with others will be successful if you follow these precepts. Think of the long term and don't act impulsively for any perceived short-term advantage or out of provocation. By keeping faith with what is true and remaining honest, as you proceed towards your goal, you are guaranteed to be successful. If you go against your intuition or your conscience, you will fail.

Judgement

It will be advantageous to be firm and correct. There will be free course and success. Let one also nourish a docility like that of a cow, and there will be good fortune.

Be calm and humble and remain committed to what you believe to be right and true.

Interpretation

Both primary trigrams represent fire and light, the sun as the source of all light, and its illuminating radiance. It is the symbol for intelligence.

Image

Brightness everywhere. The wise man cultivates more and more his brilliant virtue, and diffuses its brightness over the four quarters of the land.

Don't hoard your wisdom, but use it for the benefit of all.

Line readings

Line 1: *One is ready to move with confused steps. But if one treads reverently at the same time, there will be no mistake.*

Keep calmly and consistently to the path of truth and rightness, and resist any attempts to make you deviate from this.

Line 2: *One is in one's place in yellow. There will be great good fortune.*

Everything is favourable and going well.

Line 3: *One is in a position like that of the declining sun. Instead of playing on his instrument of earthenware, and singing to it, he utters the groans of an old man of eighty. There will be misfortune.*

'What will be, will be': don't worry or grieve over the future or your own mortality.

Line 4: *How abrupt it is, as with fire, with death, to be rejected by all!*

Don't waste your energies on short-lived ventures.

Line 5: *One flows with torrents of tears, and groans in sorrow. There will be good fortune.*

Don't succumb to downheartedness. Keep looking clearly towards your goal and remain humble and persevering. Be heartened by the concern of others and spare some of your thoughts and concern for them.

Line 6: *The king employs one in his punitive expeditions. Achieving admirable merit, one breaks only the chiefs of the rebels. Where his prisoners were not their associates, he does not punish. There will be no error.*

Although you still have faults despite your laudable attempts to remove all faults, it is praiseworthy that you own to them, though they are not great. Retain your strength and generosity, particularly to those you are competing with.

**Hexagram 31
Hsein—Courtship**

Component Trigrams

Primary: Tui—Marsh (upper), Ken—The Mountain (lower). Nuclear: Ch'ien—Heaven (above), Sun—The Wind (lower).

Keywords

Lake, mountain, reciprocity, objectivity, emptiness, correct mutual assistance.

Commentary

In the situation in which you find yourself, being sensitive and bringing to bear a proper influence which will result in a worthy end will successfully resolve the situation. Your influence should not be purposive or self-seeking, but selfless, passive and benign. Nevertheless, this position will lead to reward and mutual benefit for you and others. You must cultivate keeping an open mind and a responsiveness which will immediately instigate the right and appropriate action for any circumstance.

Judgement

There will be free course and success. It will be advantageous to be firm and correct. In marrying a young lady, there will be good fortune.

Responsiveness and influence are reciprocated by another. Be sensitive to the needs of the other and remain inwardly calm even when you are outwardly excited and happy.

Interpretation

On a mountain there is a lake; it conforms to the mountain and the mountain obtains rain from the clouds for the lake. The hexagram is about reciprocal relationships and self-less mutual influence. The primary trigrams also signify young women and men in courtship, with their selfless concern for each other and their harmonious relations.

Image

A lake on top of a mountain. The wise man keeps his mind free from preoccupation, and open to receive the influences of others.

The wise man knows that he still has everything to learn, and is always open to new ideas and fresh perspectives. You should remember that you still have much to learn from others and should humbly strive to emulate the example of the wise man.

Line readings

Line 1: *One moves only one's great toes.*

You need to consider the changes you must make to yourself in order to proceed in your direction, from minor changes to more radical. For the time being others will be unaware of your intention to change.

Line 2: *One moves the calves of one's legs. There will be misfortune. If one abides quiet in one's place, there will be good fortune.*

This is not the time for making changes or for action. You must wait otherwise you will fail.

Line 3: *One moves one's thighs, and keeps close hold of those whom one follows. Going forward in this way will cause regret.*

Seeking to use your influence for selfish ends is wrong. You must reeducate your thinking, and clarify your thoughts.

Line 4: *Firm correctness will lead to good fortune, and prevent all occasion for repentance. If one be unsettled in one's movements, only one's friends will follow one's purpose.*

Keep a clear mind and course and follow the promptings of your intuition and your conscience. Don't try to manipulate situations and others for your own advantage.

Line 5: *One moves the flesh along the spine above the heart. There will be no occasion for repentance.*

You must be more flexible and less rigid in your approach and ideas. You will gain approval and respect from others.

Line 6: *One moves one's jaws and tongue.*

'All talk and no action': you must avoid gaining this unenviable reputation. It is better to let your correct and worthy actions speak for you.

Hexagram 32
Heng—Persistence

Component Trigrams

Primary: Chen—Thunder (upper), Sun—Wind (lower). Nuclear: Tui—Marsh (above), Ch'ien—Heaven (below).

Keywords

Thunder, wind, perseverance, persistence, commitment, endurance, constancy.

Commentary

You should persevere on your chosen path, confident in its rightness. Maintain your responsibilities and everything will be fine.
You must be sure what your function is and act accordingly,
whether it is to be a faithful follower or a conscientious leader. At
the end of your chosen path is success and a new beginning.

Judgement

There will be successful progress and no error. Advantage will
come from being firm and correct. Movement in any direction
whatever will advantageous.

Change is a fact in our lives and we must be responsive to it
and change accordingly. But there should always remain at the
heart of all our changes an unchanging core of meaning.

Interpretation

The images of thunder and wind convey the ideas of moving, involving and enduring. The primary trigrams signify eldest son
and eldest daughter, and symbolize a long and harmonious marriage. Using the wisdom gained from the lessons of the past to live
more successfully in the present is the message of the hexagram.

Image

Thunder and wind. The wise man stands firm, and does not
change his method of operation.

Be flexible in the face of change but be steadfast in your commitment to your direction.

Line readings

Line 1: *One is deeply desirous of long continuance. Even with
firm correction there will be misfortune; there will be no advantage in any way.*

An impetuous act has altered your course and you have lost
touch with your past and a sense of direction towards your future.
Taking on too much too soon leads to failure.

Line 2: *All occasion for repentance disappears.*

Learn to be guided by your intuition and know your limitations.

Line 3: *One does not continuously maintain one's virtue. There
are those who will impute this to one as a disgrace. However firm
one may be, there will be grounds for regret.*

Your actions have led you into situations where you have felt publicly embarrassed. You must learn to be more robust in such situations and not let them get to you. Use any such occasion as an opportunity to learn something valuable for yourself.

Line 4: *A field where there is no game.*

You must be clearheaded and clearsighted in order to deal with difficulties: only then can you make valid and worthwhile decisions.

Line 5: *One continuously maintains the indicated virtue. In a wife this will be fortunate; in a husband, unfortunate.*

In any union or partnership you should be flexible and be prepared, if necessary, to depart from custom and convention as a response to changing situations. But never adapt to the point of losing touch with your true self.

Line 6: *One excites oneself to long continuance. There will be misfortune.*

'More haste, less speed': hurry and constant activity are wasteful and harmful. Measured and thoughtful progress towards your goal is more efficient and more likely to succeed.

Hexagram 33
Tun—Withdrawal

Component Trigrams

Primary: Ch'ien—Heaven (upper), Ken—The Mountain (lower).
Nuclear: Ch'ien—Heaven (above), Sun—Wind (below).

Keywords

Heaven, the mountain, poise, strategic retreat, persistence, endurance, unfavourable forces.

Commentary

Heaven moves upwards in response to increasing power; it is time for strategic retreat. With threatening forces ranged against you, your success in mitigating their harmful effects depends on the timing and the direction of your withdrawal. You have to proceed carefully, remaining modest and virtuous in the small steps you take; this will allow you to make the best out of the situation. Be realistic and accept that you cannot defeat the forces that you face; all you can do is find the best way of accommodating them, with the least harm to yourself. You are not forsaking your path but seeking better ways of continuing on it. Avoid false and dubious characters if you can, but keep them at a safe distance if you can't. Stay away from conflict with such disruptive types. Maintain your own balance and strength and protect yourself as needs be from their adverse influence.

Judgement

There will be successful progress. To a small extent it will still be advantageous to be firm and correct.

Act economically and timeously. Fail to do this and you will lose respect and authority and encounter further conflict.

Interpretation

Heaven above, the mountain below. The hexagram signifies the superior person moving away from the inferior. When faced with overwhelming odds from a host of malicious adversaries, the virtuous person makes a strategic withdrawal.

Image

Heaven is above the mountain. The wise man keeps small men at a distance, not by showing that he hates them, but by his own dignified gravity.

One retains one's dignity and balance by withdrawing into inner contemplation.

Line readings

Line 1: *A retiring rearguard. The position is perilous. No movement in any direction should be made.*

Your retreat has been mis-timed and you are open to attack. Pause and do nothing which will provoke others.

Line 2: *One holds one's purpose fast as if by a thong made from the hide of a yellow ox, which cannot be broken.*

You must maintain strength of purpose and conviction, and show exemplary conduct, in order to endure. Be prepared to accept help from someone stronger.

Line 3: *One is retiring but bound, to one's distress and peril. To deal with one's binders as in nourishing a servant or concubine would be fortunate for one.*

Your priority is withdrawal from a dangerous situation. Those who are holding you back are compounding the danger. If they can't be enlisted to help you then you must escape from them.

Line 4: *One retires, irrespective of one's personal inclinations. In a wise man this will lead to good fortune; a small man cannot attain to this.*

Retreat is not the same as surrender. You are taking the wise course by withdrawing, and there is no need to feel guilty.

Line 5: *One retires in an admirable way. With firm correctness there will be good fortune.*

Remain committed to the course you have chosen and don't allow yourself to be diverted. Others will now see what you are doing.

Line 6: *One retires in a noble way. It will be advantageous in every respect.*

Sometimes the correct response to setbacks and disappointments is simply to move away, as you are doing now. Remain positive and optimistic in the face of unavoidable fate.

Hexagram 34
Tachuang—The power of the great

Component Trigrams
Primary: Chen—Thunder (upper), Ch'ien—Heaven (lower). Nuclear: Tui—Marsh (above), Ch'ien—Heaven (below).

Keywords
Thunder, the heavens, strength, power, influence, authority, self-restraint, propriety.

Commentary
You are in the fortunate position of being able to exercise considerable power. Use this power wisely, for the benefit of all and not just yourself. Don't get obsessed with power for its own sake, and smugly preen your own ego. Use it selflessly for good ends and make sure that you stay in harmony with yourself and those around you. Be strong of character when wielding this power, and use it correctly, and anything will be possible. If you misuse the power you have then unhappiness and failure will be the result.

Judgement

It will be advantageous to be firm and correct.

Act cautiously and prudently. Sometimes the best way forward is to pause and wait for a while.

Interpretation

An auspicious situation. Thunder resounds in the heavens: great forces are readying their strength. But this power will have to be employed with a firm sense of moral propriety if it is to be effective in achieving successful aims.

Image

Thunder in its place in heaven. The wise man does not take a step which is not according to propriety.

You must be a moral exemplar at this time, so avoid dubious company and don't deviate from the worthy course you have chosen.

Line readings

Line 1: *One manifests one's strength. But advance will lead to misfortune, most certainly.*

Don't rush into action as this will result in failure.

Line 2: *With firm correctness there will be good fortune.*

Things are beginning to go well so continue with the same commitment, without slacking off.

Line 3: *The small man uses all his strength; the wise man's rule is not to do so. Even with firm correctness the position would be perilous. A ram butts against a fence and gets his horns entangled.*

Things may going well but exercise restraint. Don't charge ahead regardless.

Line 4: *Firm correctness leads to good fortune, and occasion for repentance disappears. The fence opens without the horns being entangled. Strength like the wheel-spokes of a large waggon.*

Follow through with your intentions. The effectiveness of your power depends on your motives. Take time to sort them out.

Line 5: *One loses one's ram-like strength in the ease of one's position. But there will be no occasion for repentance.*

Doing something about the negative aspects of your character is a good thing. Exercise tolerance.

Line 6: *A ram butts against the fence and is unable either to re-*

treat, or to advance as he would fain do. There will not be advantage in any respect; but if one realizes the difficulty of one's position, there will be good fortune.

Avoid overreaching yourself; you risk coming up against something that will halt your progress. If you are already in a deadlock situation, then back away.

Hexagram 35
Chin—Advancement

Component Trigrams

Primary: Li—Fire (upper), K'un—Earth (lower). Nuclear: K'an—Water (above), Ken—The Mountain (below).

Keywords

Sunrise, earth, shining brilliance, clarity, accumulating virtue.

Commentary

You luckily find yourself in the right place at the right time and have the opportunity, perhaps with the help of influential people, of furthering your plans and taking action which will achieve great success. It is a favourable time for partnerships and you should seek one with a sympathetic authoritative person. Your joint venture has considerable potential for substantial benefits for you. You should go all out and aim for the heights during this highly auspicious period of change and growth. Keep your integrity, and the full potential of your talents and character will almost effortlessly be realized during this time.

Judgement

A prince secures tranquillity for his people. The king presents him with numerous horses. Three times in one day he is received at interviews.

A good leader only takes others with him if he has their respect and loyalty. He earns this by his desire to act for their welfare.

Image

The bright sun rising above the earth. The wise man gives himself to make more brilliant his bright virtue.

The wise man remains committed always to the path of light and truth, disdaining the shallow and futile temptations of the material world.

Line readings

Line 1: *One wishes to advance but is kept back. Let one be firm and correct, and there will be good fortune. If trust be not reposed in one, let one maintain a large and generous mind, and there will be no error.*

Don't let yourself be upset by minor setbacks. If you remain calm and committed you may also inspire others to your cause.

Line 2: *One advances and yet one is sorrowful. If one be firm and correct, there will be good fortune. One will receive this great blessing from a kind and generous ruler.*

You feel that barriers are being put between you and the person who can help you. Maintain your strength of purpose and consider other tactics.

Line 3: *One is trusted by all around one. All occasion for repentance will disappear.*

Entering into a partnership is a good idea at this time.

Line 4: *One advances like a marmot. However firm and correct one may be, the position is one of peril.*

Trying to be as inconspicuous and innocuous as you can is not the way to proceed.

Line 5: *All occasion for repentance disappears. But let one not concern oneself about failing or succeeding. To advance will be fortunate, and in every way advantageous.*

Don't be so concerned with achievement. The most important thing is the worth of your character. Remain loyal to those who may be helping you at the moment, even if you are not progressing towards your goal.

Line 6: *One advances with strength. But one only uses it to punish the rebellious people of one's own city. The position is perilous, but there will be good fortune. Yet however firm and correct one may be, there will be occasion for regret.*

Don't move forward too quickly, but keep moving forward. Concentrate on husbanding your resources and energies and sticking to the path.

Hexagram 36
Ming I—Darkening of the light

Component Trigrams

Primary: K'un—Earth (upper), Li—Fire (lower). Nuclear: Chen—Thunder (above), K'an—Water (below).

Keywords

Earth, light, repression, obstruction, misfortune, honour, resolve.

Commentary

This is an inauspicious occasion. Perhaps there has been a lack of loyalty from those around you. Be wary of the malicious intent of authority figures or their lack of competence. You will only over-come any difficulties posed by an authority figure, with great effort and strength of purpose. Begin by accepting the fact of the obstacles that have been placed in your way; and then pursue a course of strengthening the virtuous aspects of your character. Show stead-fastness in the face of this adversity, and bring into play a strate-gic cunning in order to find the best way through. In times of such crisis you are entitled to use your wit in ways you would disdain at other times. Crafty ploys are acceptable survival tactics.

Judgement

It will be advantageous to realize the difficulty of the position and maintain firm correctness.

The wise thing to do in the midst of trouble and confusion is to stay calm and think clearly, bringing your own light to bear on the situation. Then with perseverance you can overcome any difficulties.

Interpretation

The light falls into the depths of the earth; the brilliance of virtue is obscure, but not blotted out. The hexagram is about the proper and effective response to situations where the light of reason and virtue is obscured.

Image

The sun sinks into the earth. The wise man conducts his manage-ment of men; he shows his intelligence by keeping it obscured.

Act cautiously and conduct yourself properly with others. Don't brag or be arrogant towards others.

Line readings

Line 1: *One flies with drooping wings. When the wise man is resolving his going away, he may be for three days without eating. Wherever he goes, the people there may speak derisively of him.*

You must face up to the problem at hand. Not doing so will bring unwanted attention from others.

Line 2: *One is wounded in the left thigh. One saves oneself by the strength of a swift horse; and is fortunate.*

Although things are bad they can still be remedied. Accept help from others and be prepared to give them help in turn.

Line 3: *One hunts in the south and captures the great chief of the darkness. One should not be eager to make all correct at once.*

Expect those you have offended to be angry. Take any opportunity to right any wrongs you have committed.

Line 4: *One enters the left side of the belly of the dark land. But one is able to quit the gate and the courtyard of the lord of darkness.*

You are in a tense and difficult situation. Stay calm and move cautiously away from it.

Line 5: *One does one's duty. It will be advantageous to be firm and correct.*

Sometimes the only way to protect yourself is to conceal your true self; but remain inwardly and steadfastly committed to that true self and its direction.

Line 6: *There is no light, but only obscurity. It had at first ascended to the top of the sky; its future shall be to go into the earth.*

Your strength, patience and faith are now rewarded as the bad times recede and the darkness is replaced by the light.

Hexagram 37
Chia Jen—Family

Component Trigrams

Primary: Sun—Wind (upper), Li—Fire (lower). Nuclear: Li—Fire (above), K'an—Water (below).

Keywords

Wind, fire, family, harmony, balance, propriety, adherence to structure.

Commentary

You are in a fortunate situation and with harmony and a due attendance to your responsibilities you can attain your desired goal. Apply yourself and avoid distractions. Work together with others and if everyone performs their allotted tasks to the best of their ability then everything will prosper. Whatever your position in this joint enterprise you should ensure that the spirit—and the letter—of harmony and coordination, especially with the course of the leader, prevails. Mutual respect and proper consultation within the group are required. If you then work to the best of your ability then things will go well.

Judgement

For the regulation of the family, what is most advantageous is that the wife be firm and correct.

Even if you are in a supporting role in a group you have responsibilities towards all the others, including the leader of the group.

Interpretation

This hexagram uses the symbol of the family. The order and harmony of the family group, with everyone performing their allotted tasks to the best of their ability, is the model for society at large. Their are moral aspects to this family coherence, in attitudes and conduct, and also the virtues of love, respect and loyalty.

Image

Wind coming forth from fire. The wise man orders his words according to the truth of things, and his conduct so that it is uniformly consistent.

Make sure there is a correspondence between what you say and what you do. Don't be a hypocrite.

Line readings

Line 1: *One establishes restrictive regulations in one's household. Occasion for repentance will disappear.*

Setting or knowing ground rules and keeping to them are the prerequisites for the growth of any joint endeavour or any relationship.

Line 2: *The wife takes nothing on herself, but in her central place attends to the preparation of the food. Through her firm correctness there will be good fortune.*

Don't be tempted to start anything new.

Line 3: *One treats the members of the household with stern severity. There will be occasion for repentance; there will be peril, but there will also be good fortune. If the wife and the children were to spend their time smirking and chattering, in the end there would be occasion for regret.*

Working towards maintaining an effective balance between the individual wishes of the group and the responsibilities they owe to the group is the best thing to do just now.

Line 4: *The wife enriches the family.*

Things are in proper harmony as you have the love and respect of others for your selflessness and fairness.

Line 5: *The influence of the king extends to one's family. There need be no anxiety; there will be good fortune.*

You are confident in your own ability, and your sense of well-being and happiness expresses itself with love and respect for others.

Line 6: *One is possessed of sincerity and arrayed in majesty. In the end there will be good fortune.*

With your growing status and influence, you should aspire to be a consistent source of stability and strength to those you are responsible to, allowing them to rely on your sense of Judgement and strength of character. Always, though, remain true to yourself, as you cannot grow without inner consistency, and the continuing harmony of the group depends on this.

Hexagram 38
K'uei—Opposition

Component Trigrams

Primary: Li—Fire (upper), Tui—Marsh (lower). Nuclear: K'an—Water (above), Li—Fire (below).

Keywords

Fire, marsh, disunity, alienation, neutrality, division, disagreement.

Commentary

There is disunity which will make it very difficult to achieve anything worthwhile. The conflict and division that you will face is only temporary, though, and harmony will eventually be restored. In the meantime keep your sights set low, attempting only small undertakings, and try to find common ground wherever you can. Respond calmly and resolutely to difficulties that arise. Act honestly and sincerely at all times and do things properly. Don't take advantage of others and make sure that no-one takes advantage of you. Remain optimistic in the face of challenges ahead, remembering that opposition will eventually be superseded by harmony.

Judgement

In small matters there will still be good success.

Don't try to sort everything out at once when things are going badly. You will get back to a harmonious situation by taking things one step at a time.

Interpretation

Fire flames upwards, water flows downwards; the opposing directions cause a state of disharmony. The hexagram is about a social state in which discord and mutual rejection are the rule. There is dissent, conflict and stalemate. It also conveys the idea of being tugged in two opposing directions. The hexagram suggests what modest steps can be taken to heal breaches.

Image

Fire above the waters of the marsh. The wise man, where there is general agreement, still admits diversity.

Retaining your integrity and freedom of thought and will are the most important things in life.

Line readings

Line 1: *Occasion for repentance will disappear. One has lost one's horses, but let one not seek for them; they will return of themselves. Should one meet with bad men, one will not err in communicating with them.*

You feel you have lost something from your life, but you should not dwell on this as it is an inevitable part of changing and growing. Look to what is new; be responsive to things that you gain as a result of change in your life. If you pursue what you feel you have lost, you will find that it just moves further away. The same applies to people who are no longer a part of your life. Avoid those who have lost their principles as you cannot change this fact.

Line 2: *One meets one's lord in a side-street. There will be no error.*

An accidental and unavoidable meeting with someone will turn out well for you. Things will change for the better as a result of this meeting with a person you may have been trying avoid.

Line 3: *One's carriage is dragged back, while the oxen in it are pushed back, and one is subjected to the shaving of one's head and the cutting off of one's nose. There is no good beginning but there will be a good end.*

You are in a stagnant situation, with no progress possible and this frustrates you. Things will improve in time. For the time being it is best to simply accept what you have and where you are.

Line 4: *One is solitary amidst the prevailing disunion. But one meets with the good man and they blend their sincere desires together. The position is one of peril, but there will be no mistake.*

You will feel less solitary and better able to manage your problems when you meet someone in a similar situation to yourself, with whom you are in tune.

Line 5: *Occasion for repentance will disappear. With one's relative and one's helper, one unites closely and readily as if one were biting through a piece of skin. When one goes forward with this help, what error can there be?*

You are fortunate as you have a sympathetic and happy relationship with an honest and sincere friend, which has ameliorated your feeling of isolation.

Line 6: *One is solitary amidst the prevailing disunion. One seems to see a pig bearing on its back a load of mud, or fancies there is a carriage full of ghosts. One first bends one's bow against him, and afterwards unbends it, for one discovers that he is not an assailant to injure, but a near relative. Going forward, one shall meet with genial rain, and there will be good fortune.*

Don't misjudge your companions as this creates unnecessary and avoidable friction and conflict. Reciprocate their honesty and sincerity and you will be able to relate to one another again.

Hexagram 39
Chien—Barriers

Component Trigrams

Primary: K'an—Water (upper), Ken—The Mountain (lower). Nuclear: Li—Fire (above), K'an—Water (below).

Keywords

Water, mountain, blockage, danger, dilemmas, caution, dangerous pathways.

Commentary

During times of danger and stalemate you must focus on the development of your true self. Fulfilling the potential of your character will give you the strength to overcome the formidable obstacles in front of you. Knowing when and when not to act is a wise capacity and you may need to develop this ability in order to deal with the present situation. Exercise caution before moving forward and seek the advice of experienced elders.

Judgement

Advantage will be found in the south-west and the contrary in the north-east. It will be advantageous also to meet with the great man. In these circumstances, with firmness and correctness, there will be good fortune.

To prepare for the proper action to deal with the difficult situation that faces you, it would be advisable to seek the necessary wisdom through meditation and the consulting of wise and experienced people.

Interpretation

Water is trapped at the top of the mountain, it cannot follow its natural course. The hexagram is about how to deal with obstructions or impediments, or possible debilitating injury. A wise equanimity is required.

Image

Water atop a mountain. The wise man turns round and examines himself, and cultivates his virtue.

Developing your insight and heightening your awareness is necessary, in order to see a way through severe difficulties and obstacles.

Line readings

Line 1: *Advance will lead to greater difficulties, while remaining stationary will afford ground for praise.*

It is better to pause and wait rather than rashly proceed, creating further problems.

Line 2: *The servant of the king struggles with difficulty on difficulty, and not with a view to his own advantage.*

You must face up to inescapable problems.

Line 3: *One advances but only to greater difficulties. One remains stationary, and returns to one's former associates.*

You are responsible to others so it would be irresponsible to act just now when that action will have consequences for others. Take time to think about the situation to find the best way of proceeding. You will then be able to move forward with renewed energy.

Line 4: *One advances but only to greater difficulties. One remains stationary, and unites with others.*

You need help from others, despite what you may think. Others are ready to help but you must ask them as they believe their help would not be welcomed by you.

Line 5: *One struggles with the greatest difficulties, while friends come to help one.*

In an attempt to help another you have become entangled in difficulties. But you can expect others to come to your aid as they saw the honesty of your motives. You will overcome the obstacles which have halted you.

Line 6: *One goes forward, only to increase the difficulties, while remaining stationary will be productive of great merit. There will be good fortune, and it will be advantageous to meet with the great man.*

Your period of withdrawal in order to meditate on your difficult situation cannot be extended indefinitely. You are not a wise man who can renounce the world and live in solitude. You should now be able to see more clearly how to proceed; so it is time to return to your difficulties and face them, unpalatable as that may be.

Hexagram 40
Chien—Removing obstacles

Component Trigrams

Primary: Chen—Thunder (upper), K'an—Water (lower). Nuclear: K'an—Water (above), Li—Fire (below)

Keywords

Thunder, rain, spring, release, growth, joy, vitality, dispersal.

Commentary

This is a propitious time. After a prolonged period of trial and obstruction a great new direction is open to you. You have a great opportunity. As all the troubles that have beset you fade away, and you approach an unprecedented time of growth and development, you are in a position to forgive and forget. The only thing you have to guard against now is failing to act boldly and timeously in progressing towards a worthy aim. Take full advantage of your fortunate circumstances.

Judgement

Advantage will be found in the south-west. If no further operations be called for, there will be good fortune in coming back to the old conditions. If some operations be called for, there will be good fortune in the early conducting of them.

You must move forward quickly on your chosen path in order to alleviate the stresses that threaten to derail you; but don't overreach yourself.

Interpretation

The hexagram suggests the tension-releasing, cleansing effect of a massive thunderstorm. The ideas of releasing pent-up power and of deliverance from constraint are suggested. It is time to move into a better future and forget the troubles of the past. But don't get carried away as your good fortune has still to arrive.

Image

Thunder and rain acting together. The wise man forgives errors and deals gently with crimes.

'Clearing the air' is necessary to resolve disputes and tensions, and come to better terms with things and people so that you can move forward. You will also be able to see more clearly the best direction for you.

Line readings

Line1: *One will commit no error.*

You can take time out from your problems and recharge your depleted batteries in peace and quiet.

Line 2: *One catches, in hunting, three foxes, and obtains the golden arrows. With firm correctness there will be good fortune.*

Be wary of those who may seek to exploit you because they see your good fortune coming. Preserve your energies and be careful.

Line 3: *A porter rides in a carriage with his burden. He will only tempt robbers to attack him. However firm and correct he may try to be, there will be cause for regret.*

Don't advertise your good fortune as there are potential dangers lurking in the circle that surrounds you. Some of your friends are deceiving you. Be careful.

Line 4: *One is instructed to remove his toes. Friends will then come, between him and them there will be mutual confidence.*

You must be realistic and sensible and confront those who are not genuine friends with the fact of your knowledge of their duplicity. Remove them from your circle, otherwise you could be faced with your genuine friends leaving.

Line 5: *The wise man executes his function of removing what is harmful, in which case there will be good fortune, and confidence in him will be shown even to the small men.*

As you move those who are undesirable from your circle of friends, so you must discard those regressive aspects of your character and achieve greater clarity of mind and grow in wisdom.

Line 6: *A prince with his bow shoots at a falcon on the top of a high wall, and hits it. The effect of his action will be in every way advantageous.*

It is best to ponder a situation and then act in due time and appropriately. But to resolve a situation it is sometimes necessary to use force.

Hexagram 41
Sun—Reduction

Component Trigrams

Primary: Ken—The Mountain (upper), Tui—Marsh (lower). Nuclear: K'un—Earth (above), Chen—Thunder (below).

Keywords

The mountain, marsh, sacrifice, restraint, self-control, discipline, attendance to excess.

Commentary

This is a time of loss, which will in turn bring gain and a new beginning. You are in a situation where it is paramount that you curb your own excesses. You will have to do whatever it takes to return your self to balance and health, in order to act correctly again. If you are sincere and unremitting in your efforts at self-improvement then you will reap the rewards. Even if the necessary improvement only needs to be small, it will be enough if it is done with genuine wholeheartedness. There must be a persistent effort to improve your character and you must avoid loss of self-control leading you into mistakes.

Judgement

If there is sincerity there will be great good fortune: freedom from error; firmness and correctness that can be maintained; and advantage in every movement that shall be made. In what shall this sincerity be employed? In sacrifice two baskets of grain may be presented, though there be nothing else.

The experience of loss can be valuable and profitable. Respond to it with sincerity and optimism.

Interpretation

The trigrams' symbolism: the marsh water below the mountain evaporates and nourishes the vegetation above. The hexagram's form suggests the image of the lower trigram of strong yang lines generously yielding its top line to the upper trigram of weak yin lines. The idea is of voluntary loss or relinquishing, curbing excess for a greater purpose, which will deliver reward.

Image

The lake below the mountain. The wise man restrains his wrath and represses his desires.

Unrestrained passions and indulgence in excess lead you into difficulties. It is time to exercise self-control and restraint.

Line readings

Line 1: *One suspends one's own affairs, and hurries away to help another. One will commit no error, but let one consider how far one should contribute what is one's own to the other.*

Use this time of restraint and lack of movement to help, modestly and humbly, those others who need it. If it is you who is seeking help, don't become a burden to others.

Line 2: *It will be advantageous to maintain a firm correctness, and action will bring no misfortune. One can give increase to another without taking from oneself.*

Don't do anything which goes against your principles. Retain your honour and dignity.

Line 3: *Three men walk together, then the number is diminished by one; and one, walking, finds his friend.*

There is conflict in your group, animosities and jealousies, resulting from there being one person in the group who should no longer be a member. This person must leave. If it is you who has to leave then it is best that you take a companion with you.

Line 4: *One diminishes the ailment under which one labours by making another hasten to one's help and make one glad. There will be no error.*

Welcome help in your efforts when it is offered. It comes from a genuine desire to contribute.

Line 5: *The ruler's subjects add to his stores ten pairs of tortoise shells, and accept no refusal. There will be great good fortune.*

This is a time of great good fortune, when you have success in everything.

Line 6: *One gives increase to others without taking from oneself.*

There will be no error. With firm correctness there will be good fortune. There will be advantage in every movement that shall be made. One will find ministers more than can be counted by their clans.

You will achieve your goals if you persist in your course with sincerity and honesty. Your genuineness will encourage others to come to your help in the spirit of friendship.

Hexagram 42
I—Increase

Component Trigrams
Primary: Sun—Wind (upper), Chen—Thunder (lower). Nuclear: Ken—The Mountain (above), K'un —Earth (below)

Keywords
Wind, thunder, reinforcement, addition, augmentation, abundance, gain.

Commentary
A highly auspicious time. You will overcome all obstacles and achieve success in your undertakings. But during your time of prosperity and success it is your responsibility and honour to share your good fortune with others. All you achieve and are granted by fortune is only to give you the opportunity to be selfless and show generosity to others by helping to improve their situations.

Judgement
There will be advantage in every movement which shall be undertaken. It will even be advantageous to cross the great stream.

You should savour your time of success and good fortune while it lasts and use it to enable you to give as much help to others as possible. In this will be true reward.

Interpretation
In the hexagram we have wind above and thunder below; each strengthens the other. Thus we derive the ideas of growth and increase. Increase is also conveyed by the donation of the yang line from the upper trigram to the lower, to strengthen it. The upper

trigram also signifies the wood from which a boat is constructed. A journey over water may feature in the good fortune which will be heaped upon you.

Image

Thunder and wind together. When the wise man sees what is good, he moves towards it; and when he sees his errors, turns from them.

Follow the moral example of the wise man and cultivate the self-awareness which will allow you to identify and eradicate the weaknesses and faults in your nature. Compare yourself objectively with the good character of others.

Line readings

Line 1: *It will be advantageous for one to make a great movement. If it be greatly fortunate, no blame will be imputed to one.*

Your position of great good fortune should encourage you to achieve great aims. Your selflessness and the selfless help of others will bring about success.

Line 2: *The people add to the rulers stores ten pairs of tortoise shells whose oracles cannot be gainsaid. Let one persevere in being firm and correct, and there will be good fortune. Let the king employ the people in presenting his offerings to God, and there will be good fortune.*

Everything in your life is in harmony and everything you do achieves success. Remember to keep to your true path in the midst of your good fortune.

Line 3: *One receives increase by misfortune, so that one shall be led to good, and be without blame. Let one be sincere and pursue the path of the Mean, so shall one secure the recognition of the ruler, like an officer who announces himself to his prince by the symbol of his rank.*

Someone is in need and you should take the opportunity to unselfishly give them help. This will bring its own rewards.

Line 4: *One pursues the due course. One's advice to one's prince is followed. One can with advantage be relied on in such a movement as that of removing the capital.*

You should take the opportunity that presents itself of being a mediator. It is good that you are respected and trusted enough to be offered this role. Accept the responsibility with a good heart.

Line 5: *One seeks with sincere heart to benefit all below. There need be no question about it; the result will be great good fortune. All below will with sincere heart acknowledge one's goodness.*

Generosity and benevolence are exercised for their own sake and with no other motives. You will be respected for such acts.

Line 6: *None will contribute to one's increase, while many will seek to assail one. One observes no regular rule in the order of one's heart. There will be misfortune.*

It is not enough to exercise an impersonal kind of kindness and benevolence. You must open yourself genuinely to others in order to have friendships and companionship. You must give of yourself and your time to others, and not just rely on your actions.

Hexagram 43
Kuai—Displacing

Component Trigrams
Primary: Tui—Marsh (upper), Ch'ien—Heaven (lower). Nuclear: Ch'ien—Heaven (above), Ch'ien—Heaven (below).

Keywords
Marsh, heaven, threatening skies, corruption, virtue, resolve.

Commentary
You will have to do something regarding influential and powerful people who are unworthy of their positions and authority. You cannot ignore their abuses of power nor can you directly challenge them. You will have to use your own strength of character and sense of moral purpose, along with help from those who are inspired by your example, to change things for the better. Making the offences known to someone in authority who can be trusted is a worthwhile tactic, as is enlisting the public on your side. The main thing, though, is to remain convinced of the rightness of your cause and to maintain good relations with others. You should not set out to act because you have a personal axe to grind with someone.

Judgement
The culprit's guilt should be made known in the royal court, with

a sincere and earnest appeal for sympathy and support. There will be peril. One should also make announcement in one's own city, and show that it will not be well to have recourse at once to arms. In this way there will be advantage in whatever one goes forward to.

Don't use force to achieve your aim, but rely on your own virtuous character. You have to show steadfastness, honesty and strength in pursuing this worthwhile course.

Interpretation

The marsh waters have evaporated and changed into clouds which have ascended up to the heavens. A cloudburst is imminent. The hexagram is about how you can avoid social and political storms and the disorder they create. The form of the hexagram symbolizes the inferior person in a position of influence (the top yin line) who confronts and opposes those who are true and honest. It suggests that those of virtue will successfully resist and overwhelm the threat to them.

Image

The waters rise to heaven. The wise man bestows reward on those below him, and dislikes allowing his gifts to accumulate undispensed.

Be flexible and cultivate self-awareness in order to remedy your faults.

Line readings

Line 1: *One advances in the pride of one's strength. One goes forward, but will not succeed. There will be ground for blame.*

Know your limitations and be cautious with any new undertaking.

Line 2: *One is full of apprehension and appeals for sympathy and help. Late at night hostile measures may be taken against one, but one need not be anxious about them.*

If you remain wary and anticipate problems before they appear then you will be able to deal confidently with them.

Line 3: *One is about to advance with strong and determined looks. There will be misfortune. But the wise man, bent on cutting off the criminal, will walk alone, and encounter the rain, till he be hated by his proper associates as if he were contaminated by the others. In the end there will be no blame against him.*

Keeping to your own true path and remaining calm and in control is the best way to conduct yourself, when you are isolated and surrounded by the animosity, the malicious gossip and calumny of others.

Line 4: *One has been punished by whipping, and one walks slowly and with difficulty. If one could act like a sheep led after its companions, occasion for repentance would disappear. But though one hear these words, one will not believe them.*

This is an inauspicious time to try and move forward. Remain where you are and don't stubbornly reject advice.

Line 5: *The small men are like a bed of weeds, which ought to be uprooted with the utmost determination. Having such determination, one's action, in harmony with one's central position, will lead to no error or blame.*

You cannot eradicate all evil in the world. You must live with this realization. What you can do successfully and continually is promote the power of good.

Line 6: *One has no helpers on whom to call. One will end with misfortune.*

Be extra-vigilant with yourself when it seems that you have achieved your purpose and the bad times are finally over. Don't become blase. What to do with victory can be a great responsibility and the situation demands the right thought and action.

Hexagram 44
Kou—Encountering

Component Trigrams

Primary: Ch'ien—Heaven (upper), Sun—Wind (lower). Nuclear: Ch'ien—Heaven (above), Ch'ien—Heaven (below).

Keywords

Wind, heaven, pernicious influences, temptation, corruption, encroachment.

Commentary

There are strong influences for the good at work in your life but you should still be careful in your choice of those who work with you and for you; be alert for negative influences at work among them that are likely to stir up trouble. There is a weak negative force attempting unsuccessfully at the moment to affect your life, but if you ignore it, it could become more effective. Try to prevent anyone of doubtful or bad character getting the chance to exert any influence. If they do they will draw others into their fold and cause your fortunes to gradually diminish. If you act swiftly and boldly you will be able to prevent such a decline. But if you hesitate or try to elaborate a plan, then the negative forces will entrench themselves and prosper to your disadvantage.

Judgement

A female who is bold and strong. It will not be good to marry such a female.

Those of poor character attain positions of influence because those of good character allow themselves to be duped. They support bad characters who present themselves as innocent and reliable.

Interpretation

The upper trigram, representing royalty, uses the penetrating power of the wind. The image is of a prince's will being taken to all corners of the land. The single yin line at the bottom signifies a harmful force in a futile attempt to get into the situation.

Image

Wind below heaven. The ruler delivers his charges, and promulgates his announcements throughout the four corners of the kingdom.

It is better and wiser to delegate responsibilities to others, thus gaining respect for the soundness of your leadership.

Line readings

Line 1: *One should be like a carriage tied and fastened to a metal drag, in which case with firm correctness there will be good fortune. But if one move in any direction, misfortune will appear. One will be like a lean pig, which is sure to keep jumping about.*

Irrespective of the forces or obstacles there may be against you, you should keep resolutely going forward on your chosen path.

Line 2: *One has a wallet of fish. There will be no error. But it will not be well to go forward to the guests.*

Your lack of progress and your feelings of frustration are the

result of your own actions. You must suppress your frustrated feelings as expressing them at this time will cause you problems.
Line 3: *One has been punished by whipping and walks with difficulty. The position is perilous, but there will be no great error.*

By shrewdly anticipating likely difficulties you are better able to deal with them when they arrive. Retain your self-control and equanimity and don't give way to anything you disagree with.
Line 4: *One has one's wallet, but no fish in it. This will give rise to misfortune.*

Don't make the mistake of cutting yourself off from people because you have attained a position of power. You still need these people. Alienate them now and you would have no-one if you were deposed from your present position.
Line 5: *A medlar tree overspreads the gourd beneath it. If one keeps one's brilliant qualities concealed, a good issue will descend as from heaven.*

If you remain virtuous in your character and path, then you will have good fortune. Be content in yourself. All you have to impress on others is your genuine concern for them.
Line 6: *One receives others on one's horns. There will be occasion for regret, but there will be no error.*

You have removed yourself from the situation, having done what you set out to do. Others may express antipathy and hostility to you for withdrawing. You should pay no heed as you have remained true to yourself. They will have to deal for themselves with the consequences of harbouring these negative feelings.

Hexagram 45
Ts'ui—Gathering

Component Trigrams

Primary: Tui—Marsh (upper), K'un—Earth (lower). Nuclear: Sun—Wind (above), Ken—The Mountain.

Keywords

Marsh, earth, unity, prosperity, boundaries, order, happiness, obedience.

Commentary

This is a time of unity, and efforts should be made to maintain such a state. You should enjoy and take full advantage of this favourable period. Be wary, though, of those within and without your circle who may seek from jealousy or spite to destroy your harmonious situation. You will be able at this time to draw on substantial personal and material resources. You should be willing to listen to and act on good advice from trusted and respected figures. They can help you get the most out of this time of success. Remain cautious regarding threats to your situation. But with the cooperation of others you will be able to look forward to great rewards.

Judgement

The king will repair to his ancestral temple. It will be advantageous also to meet with the great man; and then there will be progress and success, though the advantage must come through firm correctness. The use of great victims will conduce to good fortune; and in whatever direction movement is made, it will be advantageous.

By maintaining strength and a calm purpose you will enlist others in your propitious undertakings.

Interpretation

The upper trigram signifies happiness and the lower, obedience. The hexagram as a whole indicates an auspicious time when you gather together with others and form a harmonious and balanced group. Your calm happiness will face challenges.

Image

The waters are raised above the earth. The wise man has his weapons of war put in good repair, to be prepared against unforeseen contingencies.

A large group is open to threat, so precautions must be taken. Be on the alert.

Line readings

Line 1: *One has a sincere desire for union but is unable to carry it out, so that disorder is brought into the sphere of union. If one cries out for help to another, all at once one's tears will give place to smiles. One need not mind the temporary difficulty; as one goes forward, there will be no error.*

Put your faith and trust in a person of strong virtue and steady character, who will help you to solve your problems.

Line 2: *One is led forward by another. There will be good fortune, and freedom from error. There is entire sincerity, and in that case even the small offerings of the spring sacrifice are acceptable.*

Be guided by your intuition and if you feel in tune with a person or group then seek to bond with them.

Line 3: *One sighs after union and sighs, yet nowhere finds any advantage. If one goes forward, one will not err, though there may be some small cause for regret.*

As an outsider you are drawn to a group and wish to join it, but you are hesitant. You should approach the group and seek admission to it: you will be welcomed.

Line 4: *If one be greatly fortunate, one will receive no blame.*

Selfless work for the benefit of others will bring harmony and good fortune closer.

Line 5: *One is in the place of dignity and unites all under one. There will be no error. If any do not have confidence in one, see to it that one's virtue be great, long continued, and firmly correct, and all occasion for repentance will disappear.*

All members of a group must be open and honest with each other so that harmony can be established.

Line 6: *One sighs and weeps; but there will be no error.*

Openness, honesty, and the expression of feelings, is the way to strengthen the bonds within a group and thus strengthen the group.

Hexagram 46
Sheng—Ascending

Component Trigrams

Primary: K'un—Earth (upper), Sun—Wind (lower). Nuclear: Chen—Thunder (above), Tui—Marsh (below).

Keywords

Earth, wood, growth, fertility, patience, attentiveness, accumulating virtue, progress.

Commentary

This hexagram indicates that your fortunes are slowly improving. By making steady, small improvements in your character you will eventually overcome all obstacles to reach your goal and be honoured and lauded. Keep attending to these minor matters and your successful progress is assured.

Judgement

There will be great progress and success. Seeking to meet with the great man, one need have no anxiety. Advance to the south will be fortunate.

Everything is in your favour. There are no obstacles between you and your goal. Begin working toward it now and expect the help of others.

Interpretation

The trigrams signify earth and wood (Sun is wood, as well as wind). Specifically, a tree growing ever upwards, straight and true, from the earth to the heavens. From a small beginning as a sapling, the tree slowly persisted and grew beyond its initial obstacles into free, unhindered growth. Your slow, steady growth will emulate the tree's eventual, spectacular success.

Image

Wood grows within the earth. The wise man pays careful attention to his virtue, and accumulates the small developments of it till it is high and great.

From small acorns, great oaks grow. You must persist in your slow, steady growth like the tree, and you will become remarkably favoured.

Line readings

Line 1: *One advances upwards with the welcome of those above one. There will be great good fortune.*

Remain determined in the face of the length of the journey you have to make in order to reach your goal. You will get there, one small step at a time.

Line 2: *One's sincerity will make even the small offerings of the spring sacrifice acceptable. There will be no error.*

Although you still have a long way to go towards your goal, your honesty and sincerity winsfavour and sympathy from others.

Line 3: *One ascends upwards as into an empty city.*

There are no obstacles in your way. Make sure you are on the right path and remember that things could change and bring difficulty.

Line 4: *One is employed by the king to present his offerings on the mountain. There will be good fortune; there will be no mistake.*

This line suggests a new opportunity or the according of reward or honour.

Line 5: *One is firmly correct, and therefore enjoying good fortune; there will be no mistake.*

Although you are near your goal don't get excited or overconfident. Continue in the same, calm steady way until you reach your goal. Don't do anything different or anything impetuous.

Line 6: *One advances upwards blindly. Advantage will be found in a ceaseless maintenance of firm correctness.*

Ambition for its own sake will push on blindly and will ultimately fail. You need to have a clear goal so that you can work towards it, and then be aware that you have reached it. You must remain sincere and honest, and work hard towards your aims.

Hexagram 47
K'un—Exhaustion

Component Trigrams

Primary: Tui—Marsh (upper), K'an—Water (lower). Nuclear: Sun—Wind (above), Li—Fire (below).

Keywords

Marshes, water, scarcity, trial, self-discipline, opposition, endurance.

Commentary

The situation is hard and difficult. The usual, necessary resources for coping have been exhausted. There is no order or control. And you face a time of conflict, disorder and fatigue. You will have to be self-sufficient and improvize a way through the testing difficulties that inescapably confront you. You will have to rely on deep, inner strength and a willed determination to remain optimistic and cheerful no matter what. Others may be not be very understanding. You may have to make some material sacrifice. But if you have a worthy goal and persist in your path towards it, maintaining self-control and a sense of humour, you will survive the pressures on you, and your situation will gradually improve.

Judgement

There may yet be progress and success. For the firm and correct, the really great man, there will be good fortune. He will fall into no error. If one makes speeches, one is not heard.

Times of hardship can also be times of learning and growth. Remain optimistic and use your setbacks as salutary lessons. Follow the precept that actions speak louder than words.

Interpretation

The water is beneath the marshes. What is essential has been drained away. The two primary trigrams, representing delight and danger, taken together suggest a time of joy in the face of scarcity and adversity. The person of character and virtue will win through a perilous time by remaining in good spirits and acting correctly.

Image

The marsh drains away into a water-course. The wise man will sacrifice his life in order to carry out his purpose.

When bad fortune assails you and strips you of your resources, accept it as your fate, and concentrate on being self-sufficient.

Line readings

Line 1: *One sits in rags and despondency under the stump of a tree. One enters a dark valley, and for three years has no prospect of deliverance.*

You have given up and slumped into a debilitating depression, which makes your situation seem darker that it is. You must use your inner resources to help you find a way out of this depression.

Line 2: *One is despondent amidst wine and meat. The ruler*

comes to one's help. It will be well for one to maintain one's sincerity as in sacrificing. Active operations will lead to evil, but one will be free from blame.

You have a sufficiency but are offered even more. You are forced to think about it.

Line 3: *One is oppressed before a frowning rock. One lays hold of thorns. One enters the palace and does not see one's wife. There will be misfortune.*

You strive to go forward but seem unable to make any progress, being blocked by obstacles at every turn. Perhaps the problems stem from your attitudes or actions. Try to look at them clearly and objectively and discuss the matter with those close to you.

Line 4: *One proceeds very slowly to help another who is oppressed by the carriage adorned with metal in front of him. There will be occasion for regret, but the end all will be good.*

Your status may make you feel cut-off or superior to those who are in a less powerful situation, and perhaps this is compounded by feelings of guilt. Accept that you are only separated by the trappings of success and seek contact with them and possible help.

Line 5: *One is wounded. One is oppressed by the ministers. One is leisurely in one's movements however, and is satisfied. It will be well for one to be as sincere as in sacrificing to spiritual beings.*

You will have to wait patiently and wisely for things to gradually improve.

Line 6: *One is oppressed as if bound with creepers; or one is in a high and dangerous position and saying to oneself, 'If I move, I shall repent it.' If one repents of former errors, there will be good fortune in going forward.*

You feel held back and unable to move, but in fact it is only in your mind. Act now.

Hexagram 48
Ching—The Well

Component Trigrams

Primary: K'an—Water (upper), Sun—Wind (lower). Nuclear: Li—Fire (above), Tui—Marshes (below).

Keywords

Water, wood, community, propriety, order, nourishment.

Commentary

As a well nourishes the community that depends on it, so must your character have its own deep and lasting resources that will always sustain you. From your position of self-sufficient strength and energy you will be able to invest your energies in your community for the benefit of all. You must strive to maintain correctly the harmony of the community, and by so doing you will have success. If harmony is not maintained, there will be misfortune.

Judgement

A town may change but its wells remain unchanged. The water of a well never disappears and never receives any great increase. Those who come and go draw water from the well and enjoy the benefit. If one is about to draw water from the well, but the rope is too short or the bucket breaks, then there is misfortune.

Things change but the workings of human nature stay the same. One must be able to draw on one's inner resources, otherwise there will be an unfortunate lack.

Interpretation

Sun signifies wood as well as water. The hexagram as a whole represents a well with a bucket that brings up the life-sustaining substance from the unfailing spring. The idea communicated is that of the correct maintenance of communal resources. From the well of human nature we learn from our personal and communal pasts. It is important not to get too far away from what sustains us. Being guided in the present by your inner nature is vital, as is reflection on events in the past.

Image

Water raised by wood. The wise man comforts the people, and stimulates them to mutual helpfulness.

Working in harmony with others for the benefit of all is of the highest importance.

Line readings

Line 1: *The well is so muddy that men will not drink from it;*

neither birds nor other creatures will resort to an old well.

It is important to remain in touch with the present moment and also to retain your independence of mind and action. Over-stretching yourself for others can lead to depletion of your resources and a loss of individuality. You will also be taken for granted.

Line 2: *From a hole in the well the water escapes and flows away to the shrimps and such small creatures among the grass; the water of the well leaks away from a broken bucket.*

You deliberately and perversely have nothing to do with others because you believe you won't be able to stay in control of relations. This is a waste of your resources and assets as an individual, of your potential value to yourself and others—who respond to your disdain by ignoring you.

Line 3: *The well has been cleared out, but is not used. Our hearts are sorry for this, for the water might be drawn out and used. If the king were only of the same mind as us, both he and we might receive the benefit of it.*

Someone's valuable practical abilities are not being used. He is despondent, feeling unwanted and undervalued. He could do much good for the community.

Line 4: *The well has a well-laid lining. There will be no error.*

This is a time to make yourself your number one priority. You have to rest and recuperate, restore your energies. This is not self-ish indulgence but the correct thing to do, and others will have rely on their own resources for the present.

Line 5: *A clear limpid well, the waters of its cold spring are freely drunk.*

Another is offering something valuable to you and you may not be aware of this as yet. You should seek this person out and pay attention to them.

Line 6: *The water from the well is brought to the top, which is not allowed to be covered. This suggests the idea of sincerity. There will be great good fortune.*

There is a never-failing source of valuable learning in human nature and life. There are also deep spiritual resources in human nature which can be drawn on for the benefit of all. Be sympathetic to those who wish to learn.

Hexagram 49
Ko—Change

Component Trigrams

Primary: Tui—Marsh (upper), Li—Fire (lower). Nuclear: Ch'ien—Heaven (above), Sun—Wind (below).

Keywords

Marshes, fire, progression, appropriateness, preparation, renovation, reform.

Commentary

Dramatic and necessary change is taking place in your life, or is about to. Accept and become involved in making the required changes, but make sure they happen at the right and appropriate time. If you are working with others in a new enterprise then ensure that you bring clear-sightedness and clear-headedness to it, and supply a fund of optimism. You cannot rely on automatic support though, even for an undertaking with obvious attractions. You will have to be persuasive. Don't let the process of change unbalance your individual way of seeing and doing things. Make sure that the change is for a definite and necessary purpose, and is required at this time. Act selflessly and with honesty and sincerity when dealing with new situations.

Judgement

Only when something has been accomplished will it be believed in. There will be great progress and success. Advantage will come from being firm and correct. In that case occasion for repentance will disappear.

We must learn to accept change properly and this means learning and profiting from change. We also have to time our actions correctly and to take the right direction. It is wrong to act for materialist or self-seeking reasons. Other people must be taken into account.

Interpretation

In the trigrams, fire within the marshes means that major change is imminent. Fire evaporates water, water extinguishes fire. Li also indicates clear-sighted intelligence and Tui signifies delight. The change intimated is not a wilful, spontaneous or chance overthrow or rebellion, but a natural and inevitable change which is nevertheless well-planned and measured, and directed at a clearly defined goal.

Image

Fire within the waters of the marsh. The wise man regulates his astronomical calculations, and makes clear the seasons and times.

As the seasons change so must we, responding appropriately to what is asked of us.

Line readings

Line 1: *One is bound with the skin of a yellow ox.*

You should not enact any changes until it is the right time for them, though sometimes circumstances force you into premature change. In either case exercise patience and self-control.

Line 2: *One makes one's changes after some time has passed. Action taken will be fortunate. There will be no error.*

Being well-prepared for change will enable you to deal with it much more successfully.

Line 3: *One's action will bring misfortune. Though one is firm and correct, one's position is perilous. If the change one contemplates has been three times fully discussed, one will be believed in.*

Don't be too impetuous or too dilatory in meeting change. Proper timing is all. Consider the situation before you commit yourself to action and take on board the thoughts and advice of others.

Line 4: *Occasion for repentance disappears from one. Let one be believed in; and though one change existing ordinances, there will be good fortune.*

There are radical changes taking place. If you participate in these changes from an irreproachable moral standpoint and conduct yourself with integrity, then you will inevitably receive help from others.

Line 5: *The great man produces his changes as the tiger does when he changes his stripes. Before he divines and proceeds to action, faith has been reposed in him.*

If you make it completely clear to others what is informing the change, why it is taking place and the aim it has, then they will be glad to support it. Otherwise they will not.

Line 6: *The wise man produces his changes as the leopard does when he changes his spots, while small men change their faces and show their obedience. To go forward now would lead to evil, but there will be good fortune in abiding firm and correct.*

In the aftermath of great change, smaller changes will still reverberate for a time. You should only become involved with those that you can cope with.

Hexagram 50
Ting—The Cauldron

Component Trigrams

Primary: Li—Fire (upper), Sun—Wind (lower). Nuclear: Tui—Marsh (above), Ch'ien—Heaven (below).

Keywords

Fire, wood, order, stability, alliances, nourishment.

Commentary

You should use whatever means you can to look after, encourage and generally support those people of your circle who possess wisdom and ability, and have a significant contribution to make to the community. Be receptive to the original and creative ideas which are produced by these gifted people. Maintain correct and harmonious relations with these people of influence and status and it will be good for you. If you are offered the chance to join an influential group, do so with suitable grace and decorum. You should come significantly closer to a desired and worthy goal.

Judgement

Great progress and success.

The nourishing of the material and spiritual aspects of life are both equally important. Their health and well-being must always be attended to if wisdom and fruitfulness are to flourish.

Interpretation

In the trigrams we have wood below fire. This becomes the fire below a large cauldron. The hexagram's physical shape suggests the cauldron, with the bottom line as the legs, the three solid lines the vessel's body, the next two lines the handles and the top line the lid or cover. The cauldron is at the heart of the house and the source of all the nourishment for the household, material and spiritual. When the cauldron is replete, then all is harmony and well-being.

Image

Wood within fire. The wise man keeps his every position correct, and maintains secure the appointment of heaven.

Living in harmony with oneself and with others is the way to the light of wisdom, which the wise man uses to illuminate the world.

Line readings

Line 1: *The cauldron is overthrown and its feet turned up. But there will be advantage in its getting rid of what was bad in it. It shows us the concubine whose position is improved by means of her son. There will be no error.*

Recognition and success, power and influence are possible for even the humblest and lowliest. Look within yourself, cleanse and clarify where it is necessary.

Line 2: *The cauldron has food to be cooked in it. If one can say, 'My enemy dislikes me, but he cannot approach me,' there will be good fortune.*

You are successful and prospering and may incur the jealousy of others. Don't let this bother you or make you feel guilty. If you are true to yourself and your worthy path then you have nothing to fear, and nothing for others or yourself to accuse you of.

Line 3: *The cauldron has the places of its handles changed. One's progress is thus halted. The fat flesh of the pheasant which is in the cauldron will not be eaten. But the genial rain will come, and the grounds for repentance will disappear. There will be good fortune in the end.*

You are prevented from sharing your bounty and good fortune with others, and consequently feel frustrated and full of chagrin. But persist in your good intention and eventually the situation will change and you will be able to accomplish your task.

Line 4: *The cauldron has its feet broken; and its contents, designed for the ruler's use, are overturned and spilt. One will be made to blush for shame. There will be misfortune.*

You are feeling tense and vulnerable at the moment because

of stress and pressure. Be careful you don't crack because of it.
Line 5: *The cauldron has golden handles and rings of metal in them. There will be advantage through being firm and correct.*

Those around you can see your genuine, inner worth and merit and would like to help you, but there is something in your attitudes or conduct which prevents them from doing so. And this also makes you unable to share your good fortune with them.
Line 6: *The cauldron has carrying-rings of jade.*

The benefits of your good fortune can be shared with others.

Hexagram 51
Chen—Thunder

Component Trigrams
Primary: Chen—Thunder (upper), Chen—Thunder (lower). Nuclear: K'an—Water (above), Ken—The Mountain (below).

Keywords
Thunder, surprise, poise, movement, expansion, beginnings.

Commentary
You must make yourself aware of the dangers around you and take the necessary precautions. Maintaining your course on the right path and keeping your life and conduct in good order and discipline, is the best way to overcome the obstacles in front of you and reach your goal. You must stay determined and committed. Do not hesitate to act as the situation and your conscience prompts you. Be bold and brave and whatever comes against you, you can meet and master. If you are calm and disciplined, fully in control of yourself, then you will be able to dominate the troubled situation and even gain advantage from it.

Judgement
Ease and development. When the time of movement comes one will be found looking out with apprehension, and yet smiling and talking cheerfully. When the movement like a crash of thunder terrifies all within a hundred miles, one will be like the sincere worshipper who is not startled into letting go of his ladle and cup of sacrificial spirits.

The only thing to fear in a fearful situation, is your fear itself.
Your growth and development depend on you learning this and
taking it to heart.

Interpretation

Thunder above thunder, brings a resounding clamour. The hexagram signifies a severe sudden outburst of noise or a sudden and
shocking jolt of movement. It deals with the appropriate response
to situations of abrupt and shocking change.

Image

Thunder redoubled. The wise man is fearful and apprehensive,
cultivates his virtue and examines his faults.

Look at your inner values, your motives and conduct, and correct the faults and weaknesses that you find.

Line readings

Line 1: *When the movement approaches, one looks out and
around with apprehension, and afterwards smiles and talks
cheerfully. There will be good fortune.*

One you realize that it is not you alone who is affected by the
present circumstances your morale will improve.

Line 2: *When the movement approaches, one is in a position of
peril. One judges it better to let go the articles in one's possession,
and to ascend to a very lofty height. There is no occasion for one to
pursue the things one has let go; in seven days one will find them.*

Don't worry about any material losses you suffer because of
your present situation. Better to ask yourself if they were important anyway.

Line 3: *One is distraught amid the startling movements going on.
If these movements excite one to right action, there will be no
mistake.*

Don't let disturbing events affect your balance. For the time
being, go along with what fate decides for you, and in time you
will be able to take some positive action.

Line 4: *Amid the startling movements, one sinks supinely deeper
into the mud.*

When the situation becomes clearer, and you are able to think
more clearly about it, then you will be able to do something. In

the meantime, bide your time and be prepared to accommodate yourself a little to the circumstances you find yourself in. Don't be untrue to yourself though. Be prepared to take advantage of any early opportunities that may unexpectedly present themselves.

Line 5: *One comes and goes amid the startling movements of the time, and always in peril; but perhaps one will not incur loss, and find business which one can accomplish.*

Though others may think it folly and disapprove, there are certain actions you must undertake just now. If they are done in the right spirit and in the proper manner, you will come to no harm.

Line 6: *Amidst the startling movements of the time, in breathless dismay one looks around with trembling apprehension. If one takes action, there will be misfortune. If, while the startling movements have not reached one's own person and neighbourhood, one were to take precautions, there would be no error, though one's relatives might still speak against one.*

It would be better for your mental, emotional and spiritual balance if you withdrew into yourself just now. Among those others affected by the present turmoil there will be much strife and contention. Ignore any wounding comments about you made by those close to you.

Hexagram 52
Ken—The mountain

Component Trigrams

Primary: Ken—The Mountain (upper), Ken—The Mountain (lower). Nuclear: Chen—Thunder (above), K'an—Water (below).

Keywords

Mountain, stillness, correct action, observation, appropriate restraint of action.

Commentary

You must base all you do on the firmest and soundest principles, which will endure and guide you in all situations. Act only at the right time and do not act selfishly. After assessing the overall situation, act only in a way that accords with your particular circumstances and character. You will discover the most appropriate way, whether it be direct or indirect.

Judgement

When one's back is at rest, one loses all consciousness of self; when one walks in the courtyard and does not see any of the persons in it, there will be no error.

In calmness and stillness, we can often find what we have been looking for. Now is the time to sit in stillness.

Interpretation

Both trigrams represent the mountain, signifying great stillness. The mountain sitting immobile on the earth suggests great poise and inner resolution. The mountain also thrusts upwards from the earth to the heavens. And in its position it is an obstacle to those who want to go beyond it.

Image

A mountain within a mountain. The wise man does not go in his thoughts beyond the duties of the position in which he is.

You must direct your thoughts to yourself and your situation, and also examine your inner self.

Line readings

Line 1: *One keeps one's toes at rest. There will be no error; but it will be advantageous for one to be persistently firm and correct.*

Don't lose your strength of purpose, but be directed by your intuition if you feel unsure about a situation. Retain your patience and exercise caution.

Line 2: *One keeps the calves of one's legs at rest. One cannot help another whom one follows, and one is dissatisfied in one's mind.*

This is one of those occasions when you are unable to help someone, though you would like to. Be strong and remain true to yourself.

Line 3: *One keeps one's loins at rest and makes one's back rigid. The situation is perilous, and the heart glows with suppressed excitement.*

Being inflexible and stubborn causes problems. It may, among other things, result in self-willed as distinct from appropriate action, or being overbearing with others. Be wary of these faults, and take care to avoid being inflexible.

Line 4: *One keeps one's trunk at rest. There will be no error.*

Knowing when to act and when not to act is an attribute of wisdom. You must strive still to attain such clarity, becoming more selfless on the way. Then you will find peace.

Line 5: *One keeps one's jawbones at rest, so that one's words are all orderly. Occasion for repentance will disappear.*

Exercise caution and control over what you say, and let others contribute their comments and opinions.

Line 6: *One devotedly maintains one's restfulness. There will be good fortune.*

Tranquillity and peace are attained, a settled composure of mind and spirit. This is true harmony.

Hexagram 53
Chien—Gradually progressing

Component Trigrams

Primary: Sun—Wind (upper), Ken—The Mountain (lower). Nuclear: Li—Fire (above), K'an—Water (below).

Keywords

Wood, the mountain, patience, order, growth, steady advancement, deliberation.

Commentary

You will have to persist in a slow progress towards the attainment of real self-improvement and the ability to exercise a good influence on others. By progressing in small, successive steps you will be assured of omitting nothing important. You will also be a laudable example to others. And when you finally reach your goal you will be able to savour the sense of satisfaction and achievement. Make sure as you progress that your conduct and motives remain correct and orderly. This, in conjunction with your conscientious sense of purpose, will result in improvement for yourself and those in your close circle. Maintaining this constant effort at self-improvement on a long-term plan which does not look for short-term rewards, is no different from making steady progress to a worthy outcome that has benefits for all.

Judgement

The marriage of a young lady: good fortune. There will be advantage in being firm and correct.

Undertakings must proceed at their own particular pace, you can't just force them to proceed at your arbitrarily willed pace. This is particularly true of those undertakings involving other people. To effect your own self-improvement and heighten your awareness will also take the length of time that is required.

Interpretation

The trigrams represent a tree on top of a mountain. The tree's development is slow and gradual, and as it grows it is able to increasingly provide shade and other kinds of enrichment for its environment.

Image

A tree above a mountain. The wise man attains to and maintains his extraordinary virtue, and makes the manners of the people good.

In order to have an influence for the good on others you have to have reached a position of authority and respect, where your attitude and conduct is regarded as providing an example to be followed. These things only happen over a long period of time.

Line readings

Line 1: *The wild geese gradually approach the shore. A young officer in similar circumstances will be in a position of danger, and be spoken against; but there will be no error.*

You are setting out on a journey and will be crossing uncharted territory, with no familiar landmarks or people to guide you. You will have to progress cautiously. It would be advisable to pay attention to others who have something to say to you.

Line 2: *The wild geese gradually approach the large rocks, where they eat and drink joyfully and at ease. There will be good fortune.*

You feel more secure but the situation remains somewhat volatile and nervy. It would be a good idea to accept what other people may want to share with you.

Line 3: *The wild geese gradually advance to the dry plains. A husband goes on an expedition from which he does not return. A wife is pregnant, but will not nourish her child. There will be misfortune.*

You have been too forceful and impatient and have overstretched yourself. You are now in a precarious situation but you have no alternative but to continue forward with caution and vigilance.

Line 4: *The wild geese gradually advance to the trees. They may light on the flat branches. There will be no error.*

You find yourself in a situation that you were unprepared for, and that you are struggling to comprehend and cope with. You will have to sit tight and lay low for a while.

Line 5: *The wild geese gradually advance to the high mound. A wife for three years does not become pregnant; but in the end the natural issue cannot be prevented. There will be good fortune.*

Those in your close circle have been disturbed and unsettled by your achievements. Some are perhaps jealous and resentful and may wish to see you fail. Give them time. As you continue in your path they will become accustomed to the changes that you bring.

Line 6: *The wild geese gradually advance to the large heights beyond. Their feathers can be used as ornaments. There will be good fortune.*

Having attained your goal it is now time to turn in a new direction and aim for a new goal. You are now respected and admired by others. They are prepared to follow you and your example.

This is the beginning of favourable times for you. You can look forward to many new opportunities.

Hexagram 54
Kuei—The younger maiden marries

Component Trigrams

Primary: Chen—Thunder (upper), Tui—Marsh (lower). Nuclear: K'an—Water (above), Li—Fire (below).

Keywords

Thunder, marshes, autumn, decay, renewal, transitoriness.

Commentary

You are in a deteriorating situation when you may expect to have to face decay, shady-dealing and perhaps public scandal and disgrace. There may be turmoil and loss. Your relations with others may become frustratingly antagonistic and acrimonious. Even existing harmonious relationships may be disrupted and disordered, with painful consequences for all. Console yourself with the knowledge that these times are part of a cycle of change and will inevitably come to an end, and harmony will be restored. In the meantime you have no other recourse but to stoically endure your afflictions and sufferings as your inescapable fate.

Judgement

Action will bring misfortune and is in no way advantageous.

When a young maiden marries into a family she has to learn to adapt to and respect their ways of doing things; she cannot try and impose her own, or expect everyone to fit around her. She must be quietly observant and exercise tact, demonstrating an awareness and understanding of her position and role in the family. She has to keep in mind that she is just one individual within a greater group.

Interpretation

The trigrams represent thunder over the marshes, indicating a time of autumnal decline. They also signify eldest son and youngest daughter. The hexagram as a whole concerns a young daughter marrying of her own free choice, and before her elder sister. Both these acts were forbidden and regarded as serious challenges to the stability of the family and hence society. Also forbidden was the marriage of a young woman to an older man, as its motives were considered to be merely sensual and unstable. It is a highly inauspicious hexagram about the ending of harmonious social and political structures and practices. The hexagram conveys a sense of enormously significant and far-reaching endings and subsequent beginnings.

Image

Thunder above the waters of a marsh. The wise man having regard to the far-distant end, knows the mischief that may be done at the beginning.

When times are troubled and hard, when you suffer personal disappointments, and when you are keenly affected and afflicted by the breakdown of harmonious relations with others, the wisest attitude to adopt is one of fatalism and stoic patience, consoled and comforted by the realization that in time things will calm down and become bearable again.

Line readings

Line 1: *The younger sister is married off in a position secondary to the first wife. A person lame on one leg who yet manages to tramp along. Going forward will be fortunate.*

You are in a situation where you may be tempted to act for your own improvement, but you must restrain yourself. The wisest thing just now is to adopt a low profile: do and say nothing that will draw attention to yourself.

Line 2: *The younger sister is blind of one eye, and yet able to see. There will advantage in her maintaining the firm correctness of a solitary widow.*

You are in a relationship with someone who has disillusioned you by their attitude or behaviour towards you. Others around you are aware of this.

Line 3: *The younger sister is in a mean position. She returns and accepts an ancillary position.*

You are never satisfied with what you have. Perhaps you are pursuing an unreal ideal.

Line 4: *The younger sister protracts the time. She may be late in being married, but the time will come.*

Don't be despondent about your long-desired but unrealized hopes or ambitions. Retain your optimism and your integrity and wait patiently for your desired opportunity. It will eventually come and everything will be fine.

Line 5: *The younger sister of the king was married, but her gown was not equal to the still younger sister who accompanied her in an inferior capacity. The moon almost full. There will be good fortune.*

Those who don't jump at the first opportunity that comes their way but are prepared to wait, are often the best rewarded. Perhaps you are being too ambitious or unrealistic in what you want, and it would therefore be better to chose a more attainable goal. Your chances of success may then improve and you will find what you are looking for.

Line 6: *The young lady bears a basket, but without anything in it.*

The gentleman slaughters the sheep, but without blood flowing from it. There will be no advantage in any way.

You have to accept that you can't always satisfy the needs and desires of others or yourself. And anyway, it could be the case that something which seems valuable and desirable is in reality not that great at all.

Hexagram 55
Feng—Abundance

Component Trigrams

Primary: Chen—Thunder (upper), Li—Fire (lower). Nuclear: Tui—Marsh (above), Sun—Wind (below).

Keywords

Thunder, lightning, power, plenty, judicious action, opportunity.

Commentary

There is a powerful force for positive change in your life and you should take full advantage of it, as the auspicious period in front of you will end some time. Use good judgement in the actions you take. Settle any unresolved disagreements. This is the time to launch new undertakings designed to further your fortunes. If you run your affairs with a shrewd intelligence and a readiness to take bold action when required, then you may be able to prolong your period of prosperity beyond the time when it would otherwise have come to a natural end. In your relations with others you should demonstrate the enthusiasm and optimism appropriate to one who is enjoying success and good fortune. Don't make the serious error of seeing each new rewarding opportunity as just another added and troublesome burden. Enjoy the rare feeling of being able to tackle almost anything and make a success of it.

Judgement

There will be progress and development. When a king has reached the point of abundance, there is no occasion to be anxious through fear of a change. Let him be as the sun at noon.

Although your time of great good fortune will not last forever, yet still you can relish it and enjoy it, enriching yourself and others by so doing. Perhaps it would be wise to move in the direction of a spiritual goal, having achieved your material goals.

Interpretation

In the hexagram, thunder is above lightning. Together they convey the idea of a dramatic thunderstorm which dispels all murkiness and negativity, and results in an all-illuminating brilliance and clarity. From this we have the suggestions of fullness and abundance, and the sweeping away of all obstacles. But even such an irresistible force is subject to change in time.

Image

Thunder and lightning combine. The wise man decides cases of litigation, and apportions punishments with exactness.

It is necessary to have peace of mind and a clear and untroubled spirit to be in harmony and at one with yourself. Then you can see clearly and act judiciously.

Line readings

Line 1: *One meets with one's mate. Though both be of the same character, there will be no error. Advance will call forth approval.*

It would be a good thing to work for a time with another who has an attribute or resource that you lack. But you must remember that the partnership will be temporary and so be prepared to end it when the time comes.

Line 2: *One is surrounded by screens so large and thick that at midday one can see from them the stars. If one go and try to enlighten the ruler, one will make oneself be viewed with suspicion and dislike. Let one cherish one's feeling of sincere devotion that one may thereby move the ruler's mind, and there will be good fortune.*

Someone has deliberately and maliciously set out to 'eclipse' you and they are beginning to achieve their aim. Accept it and do nothing about it, as good will come of it.

Line 3: *One has an additional screen of a large and thick banner, through which at midday one can see the small star. In the darkness one breaks one's right arm; but there will be no error.*

There is nothing you can do except patiently wait.

Line 4: *One is in a tent so large and thick that at midday one can see from it the stars. But one meets with another, undivided like oneself. There will be good fortune.*

The situation is improving for you. You have encountered the person referred to in line one.

Line 5: *One brings around one the men of brilliant ability. There will be occasion for congratulation and praise. There will be good fortune.*

In your moment of imminent success you do not forget those who are around you. You consolidate your bonds with them and listen respectfully to them.

Line 6: *One has made one's house large, but it only serves as a screen to one's household. When one looks at one's door, it is still, and there is nobody about it. For three years no-one is to be seen. There will be misfortune.*

You cannot enjoy your just rewards as you have deliberately removed yourself from others and cannot share your good fortune with them. You are isolated and alone. This emotional and spiritual barrenness in the midst of plenty is your creation and your responsibility.

Hexagram 56
Lu—The traveller abroad

Component Trigrams

Primary: Li—Fire (upper), Ken—The Mountain (lower). Nuclear: Tui—Marsh (above), Sun—Wind (below).

Keywords

Fire, the mountain, the stranger, restraint, exclusion, humility.

Commentary

You should not look for any lasting outcomes or rewards from your present situation. It is only a temporary place for you and you will not be able to change your status as an outsider. If you maintain your modesty and integrity, though, you will come to no harm and will remain on target for your goal. Rely on your inner strength to see you through the present difficulties, and accept the fact that you will make little headway towards your chosen goal during this time. Don't try to force any issues or try to impose yourself on the situation. Instead of trying to combat your unsatisfactory status as an outsider, focus instead on your own virtues and qualities and learn to appreciate what can be gained from your condition of solitariness.

Judgement

There may be some little attainment and progress. If the stranger or traveller be firm and correct as he ought to be, there will be good fortune.

A selfless regard for those he meets as he passes is a worthy and admirable quality in a traveller. His small kindnesses will have a greater reward.

Interpretation

In the trigrams, fire burns on the mountain. The mountain is immobile but the fire moves around in every direction, with no fixed aim. The image suggest is that of the traveller, who is a stranger in a strange land. The trigrams move in opposite directions—the fire burns upwards, and the mountain forces downwards—and this indicates that the contact between them will be of a temporary nature. However, things can still be learned as one moves around, even if one is not explicitly promoting progress towards an aim.

Image

Fire atop the mountain. The wise man exerts his wisdom and caution in the use of punishments and not allowing litigations to continue.

If you find you have to judge others, try to do it as quickly and as objectively as possible, showing fair-mindedness.

Line readings

Line 1: *The stranger is mean and meanly occupied. It is thus that he brings on himself further calamity.*

To waste time on things which are of no importance is to squander opportunities for making progress towards a worthwhile goal Line 2: *The stranger occupies his lodging-house, carrying with him his means of livelihood, and is provided with good and trusty servants.*

Wherever he is a wise man has a clarity of self-knowledge,

never feels lost to himself. He is always true to himself. No matter where he finds himself, he can rely on his own inner resources and remain calm and truly himself.

Line 3: *The stranger burns his lodging-house and loses his servants. However firm and correct he try to be, he will be in peril.*

If you try to get involved in something which doesn't really concern you, you will get your fingers burned. Exercise self-restraint and discipline. Perhaps your friends don't seem to be in tune with you at the moment. Be patient and they will join you once again.

Line 4: *The traveller is in a resting-place, and has also the means of livelihood and the axe, but is still saying, 'I am not at ease in my mind.'*

If you seem to have resolved the difficulties and problems that have been bothering you, be cautious. This is only a temporary respite and you cannot rely on it. You must look for real and permanent answers to your difficulties.

Line 5: *One shoots a pheasant. One will lose one's arrow, but in the end will obtain praise and a high position.*

Even though you are among new and unknown people you will be able to establish a rapport or a working accord with them. This helps you feel more secure.

Line 6: *A bird burns its nest. The stranger first laughs, then cries out. He has lost his ox-like docility too readily and too easily. There will be misfortune.*

You have relaxed your self-discipline and restraint in this situation and acted unwisely, with painful and upsetting consequences for yourself and others. You have behaved like a fool and shown a lack of respect for other people. What's done is done, you cannot undo it. All you can do is find ways of coping and dealing with the situation you have created.

Hexagram 57
Sun—Wind

Component Trigrams

Primary: Sun—Wind (upper), Sun—Wind (lower). Nuclear: Li—Fire (above), Tui—Marsh (below).

Keywords

wind, gentle, repetition, penetration, communication, authority, subtlety, harmony, obedience.

Commentary

In order to succeed in a worthy aim you will have to be persistent, and seek to exercise your influence on others. Others will be necessary to help you overcome any problems. You will have to make fully clear to others what you require of them, repeating your instructions if necessary, so that they can understand and fulfil your wishes. It may not be easy to communicate what you want, but if others don't understand you and your project is stymied then the fault is yours, not theirs. It may be a good idea to call on the help of someone more experienced who you respect and value. Tactics such as emphasizing your status or prestige or trying to insist on your authority in order to bring others to do what you want, will merely be futile gestures. You will have to concentrate, and be resourceful in finding ways to get your message across and your intention fulfilled. You also have to ensure that the message you are sending out is the one that is being received. If you succeed in effective communication and are given relevant and useful help, then you will make some moderate progress.

Judgement

There will be some little attainment and progress. There will be advantage in movement in any direction whatsoever. It will be advantageous to see the great man.

Chose your goal and persevere towards it with unfailing calmness, gentleness and humility, and you will succeed. Seeking guidance from a wiser person would be good for you.

Interpretation

Wind is represented in the upper and lower trigrams. Two attributes of wind are gentleness and penetration. The topic of the hexagram is the persistent, pervasive and penetrating power of influence that a superior has over his subordinates; their obedience to his will—like a blade of grass that bends before a strong wind. The hexagram emphasizes the need for subtlety and repetition as required, in our efforts to get others to do our bidding. There must be thoughtfulness and intelligence in communications with subordinates; and assignments and tasks delegated by a superior should be faithfully implemented.

Image

Winds following each other. The wise man reiterates his orders and secures the practice of his affairs.

In order to exercise your influence effectively it may be better to consult with your own inner wisdom or seek the wise help of another, before you attempt to do anything with other people.

Line readings

Line 1: *Now one advances, now one recedes. It would be advantageous of one to have the firm correctness of the brave soldier.*

Don't vacillate. Decide promptly what you want and then set out immediately to achieve it.

Line 2: *One is beneath a couch, and employs diviners and exorcists in a way bordering on confusion. There will be good fortune and no error.*

You must find out what malicious or malevolent level of activity or plotting is going on behind closed doors and who are the perpetrators or plotters. Obtain help from others who are experienced and capable of dealing with such a situation.

Line 3: *One penetrates only by violent and repeated efforts. There will be occasion for regret.*

Now is not the time to wait and give something further thought. You must act now or you will live to regret it.

Line 4: *All occasion for repentance has passed away. One takes game for its threefold use in one's hunting.*

Maintaining your integrity and self-respect, and the correctness of your motives and conduct, will give you the peace of mind and the strength to help others.

Line 5: *With firm correctness there will be good fortune. All occasion for repentance will disappear, and all one's movements will be advantageous. There may have been no good beginning, but there will be a good end. Three days before making any changes, let one give notice of them; and three days after, let one reconsider them. There will thus be good fortune.*

If things aren't going well then it is time to stop and think about the situation and decide on the best action to take in order to remedy it. After acting you should then assess the results. If you haven't fully achieved what you set out to do, no matter. You have done your best for the time being and it is time to move on.

Line 6: *One is beneath a couch, having lost the axe with which one executed one's decisions. However firm and correct one may try to be, there will be misfortune.*

Be very careful. You have overreached yourself and become too involved in a very dark and disturbing situation. Withdraw from it without delay as it is a threat and a danger to you, and you do not have the experience to deal with it or the necessary resources to protect yourself.

Hexagram 58
Tui—The delighted

Component Trigrams

Primary: Tui—Marsh (upper), Tui—Marsh (lower). Nuclear: Sun—Wind (above), Li—Fire (below).

Keywords

Marsh, serenity, contentment, satisfaction, freedom from anxiety and doubt.

Commentary

This is an auspicious hexagram. Your are in harmony with yourself, materially and spiritually, and have an honest integrity that makes you true to yourself and others. You have need, have no use, for negative or fearful thoughts and feelings. In your relations with others be generous, modest and sincere and strive to comprehend and sympathize with their troubles and worries. If you are able to do all this with true joy, you will experience serene happiness and will be well-equipped to overcome any obstacles you come across.

Judgement

There will be progress and attainment. It will be advantageous to be firm and correct.

Through strength of purpose, persistent effort, and faithfulness to the integrity of one's true nature, you have attained harmony and happiness and are an example and a willing source of guidance to others.

Interpretation

The hexagram has the trigram Tui as both primary trigrams. It represents peaceful water as in a marsh or a lake, and suggests delight and joy. The hexagram signifies a state of serene happiness that consists of a sense of personal wholeness and well-being, and the best of relations with others. The hexagram does not wholly exclude the presence or possibility of adversity, but its concern is to emphasize the all-powerful and ultimately all-conquering human faculty of chosing to live joyfully, no matter what the circumstances.

Image

A double lake. The wise man encourages the conversation of friends and the stimulus of their common practice.

Mutual and reciprocal influence and help, brings reward and happiness.

Line readings

Line 1: *The pleasure of inward harmony. There will be good fortune.*
You are happy with your circumstances and achievements.
Line 2: *The pleasure arising from inward sincerity. There will be good fortune. Occasion for good fortune will disappear.*
Treat others with sincere respect and don't flaunt or gloat over your successes.
Line 3: *One brings round oneself whatever can give pleasure. There will be misfortune.*
You are not nourishing or cultivating your inner self, seeming to be shallowly content with superficial, material sources and means of pleasure. You will lose touch with yourself and lose your way completely unless you mend your ways.
Line 4: *One deliberates about what to seek one's pleasure in, and one is not at rest. One borders on what would be injurious, but there will be cause for joy.*
You are unhappy because you are putting everything in your

life under an analytical microscope. Open your eyes and life to
the higher things above. Set yourself to achieve the highest goals.
Line 5: *One trusts in another who would injure one. The situation
is perilous.*

Your situation is becoming vulnerable and there is a strong
likelihood that you will be exploited. Be vigilant and cautious.
Line 6: *One's pleasure leads and attracts others.*

To revel in pleasure for its own sake is dangerous. It leads
eventually to an enervating sense of boredom and restless dissat-
isfaction. You have lost touch with yourself and your sense of direction. You must restore your self-discipline and sense of purpose. Only then can you experience true delight.

Hexagram 59
Huan—Dispersal

Component Trigrams
Primary: Sun—Wind (upper), K'an—Water (lower). Nuclear:
Ken—Mountain (upper), Chen—Thunder.

Keywords
Wind, water, division, dissipation, piety, righteousness, order,
correct action.

Commentary
There are disruptive influences at work but if you adopt the right
attitude and conduct you will be able to resist these influences
and maintain proper order. You must apply yourself to attaining a
worthy goal and cultivating a virtuous character and you will
have the ability to overcome any threats to stability and harmony.
Seek help and guidance from the wisdom of your elders. It may
be necessary for you to commit yourself to a large and perilous
enterprise. As long as you act with sincerity and honesty, and remain true to your principles, there will be no danger to you.

Judgement
There will be progress and success. The king goes to his ancestral

temple; it will be advantageous to cross the great stream. It will be advantageous to be firm and correct.

Seeking spiritual union with others who share your spiritual concerns and attributes is the way to overcome problems. Cooperation and harmonious relations is the way forward.

Interpretation

In the hexagram there is wind above water, and the water ripples and disperses. The hexagram cautions against the spreading and cumulative effects of an individual or a group's divergence from the right and true course. These aimless and divisive forces can be combated by an honest and sincere commitment to worthy aims. Persevering in this course will restore proper order. The upper trigram also signifies wood, which suggests the boat that will be used to 'cross the great stream': carry out a crucial task.

Image

Wind moves above the water. The ancient kings presented offerings to God and established the ancestral temple.

Individuals can become isolated from each other and their own spiritual natures. They must come together as a people with one spiritual purpose; this will truly unite them.

Line readings

Line 1: *One is engaged in rescuing from the impending misfortune, and having the assistance of, a strong horse. There will be good fortune.*

You must do something about the conflict and confusion around you. If you don't act promptly the situation will get even more complicated and difficult too solve.

Line 2: *Amid the confusion, one hurries to one's contrivance for security. All occasion for repentance will disappear.*

You are taking a good look at yourself and don't like what you see. You must make the effort and cultivate the self-discipline to correct what is at fault in your character and principles.

Line 3: *One discards any regard for one's own person. There will be no occasion for repentance.*

Jettisoning unnecessary personal needs and wants is a good and worthy thing to do.

Line 4: *One scatters the different parties in the state; which leads to good fortune. From the dispersion he collects again good men standing out, a crowd like a mound, which is what ordinary men would not have thought of.*

Withdrawing from those around you will allow you to concentrate on the task in hand and bring it to a successful conclusion. It also permits you a clearer view of your companions and allows you to make sounder judgements about them.

Line 5: *Amidst the dispersion, one issues great announcements as the perspiration flows from one's body. One scatters abroad also the accumulations in the royal granaries. There will be no error.*

You are the linchpin of others' cooperative efforts, a focal point of ideas and inspiration for correcting the faults of the past. This is a good position.

Line 6: *One disposes of one's bloody wounds, and goes and separates oneself from one's anxious fears. There will be no error.*

You must pull back from the activities and concerns that you have been so wholeheartedly and enthusiastically involved in, as you are getting carried away and losing sight of yourself and your aims. You need a sobering respite and a chance to rediscover yourself and your priorities.

Hexagram 60
Chieh—Restraint

Component Trigrams

Primary: K'an—Water (upper), Tui—Marsh (lower). Nuclear: Ken—The Mountain (above), Chen—Thunder (below).

Keywords

Water, marshes, regulation, proper restraint, moderation, time, regular division.

Commentary

This is a situation where observing restraint and self-imposed limitations will be necessary in order to avoid the dangers caused by lack of control and poor judgement. Moderation, flexibility and appropriateness must be the watchwords. You must apply con-

straints to your dealings with others which are appropriate to the
circumstances and help to maintain good order and relations. You
will have to monitor the distribution of resources, fine-tuning
when necessary to cope with changes in the situation. Rigid adherence to strict rules and regulations will be ineffectual and will
only serve to encourage a destructive and self-defeating lack of
thought and judgement. If a certain amount of sensible flexibility
is promoted, concerning adherence to established standards, then
you will meet with success in your undertakings. But if you rely
on the unthinking application of familiar procedures then you
will be severely disillusioned. Be moderate and show good
judgement in your relations with others and you will progress.

Judgement

There will be progress and attainment. If the limitations are severe and difficult, they should not be made permanent.

Constraints and limitations are necessary for balance and good
order. But there must be moderation and flexibility. Wise discernment and judgement are required.

Interpretation

In the trigram structure there is water above marshes. If the marsh
is allocated too much water it will flood and overflow; if it receives too little water it will dry up. The concept of the hexagram
is proper regulation, sensitive restraint and ordered distribution.
The lines of the hexagram reproduce the pattern of the joints on a
bamboo stalk. This also contributes to the idea of standardized
rules and necessary limitation. The hexagram teaches about the
correct application of regulatory power in dealing with people
and allocating resources.

Image

Water fills the lake. The wise man constructs his methods of number-
ing and measurement, and discusses points of virtue and conduct.

You have to discover for yourself your limitations. Exceeding
your limitations is a waste of time and energy and ends in failure.

Line readings

Line 1: *One does not quit the courtyard outside one's door. There
will be no error.*

This is not the time to act. You should look within yourself for answers you seek, and when the time comes to act, you will know it.

Line 2: *One does not quit the courtyard inside one's gate. There will be misfortune.*

Grasp opportunities when they present themselves. You may not get a second chance.

Line 3: *One does not observe the proper regulations, in which case one shall lament. But there will be no-one to blame but oneself.*

You have shown no moderation and have wallowed in excess. You are now feeling responsible and remorseful. You realize the harm caused by exceeding your limitations and abandoning restraint.

Line 4: *One is quietly and naturally attentive to all regulations. There will be progress and success.*

You must learn to be able to calmly take the moderate path of sensible and comfortable restraint, creating a reservoir of energy for yourself.

Line 5: *One sweetly and acceptably enacts one's regulations. There will be good fortune. The onward progress with them will afford ground for admiration.*

Make sure that the limitations you set yourself or others observe the needs of the individual as well as the needs of the situation.

Line 6: *One enacts severe and difficult regulations. Even with firmness and correctness there will be misfortune. But though there be cause for repentance, it will by and by disappear.*

You have been too severe on yourself or others. Relax a little.

Hexagram 61
Chung Fu—The truth within

Component Trigrams

Primary: Sun—Wind (upper), Tui—Marsh (lower). Nuclear: Ken—The Mountain (above), Chen—Thunder (below).

Keywords

Wind, marshes, truth, transformation, flawlessness, deliberation, wisdom, humility.

Commentary

This is a highly auspicious time for your spiritual development. Cultivate the strength and power of your inner self and you will be able to accomplish any difficult undertaking. If there is such an undertaking at hand you should tackle it now, applying yourself to it with confidence in the worthiness of your aims and the integrity of your character. Your ultimate aim will not be to impose yourself on others but to become as humble and selfless as possible, and move forward with great sincerity and honesty on the right path.

Judgement

The truth within moves even pigs and fish, and leads to good fortune. There will be advantage in crossing the great stream. There will be advantage in being firm and correct.

There is great power and influence in the inner virtues of truth and sincerity. You can reach and communicate with the different inner natures of individuals, and can unite them in harmony to cooperate in the accomplishment of a great undertaking, which will have a favourable outcome.

Interpretation

The hexagram's structure has wind above the marsh. The wind penetrates in all directions and refreshes and energizes the collected waters of the marsh. Even secret and cloistered things are reached by the wind's power. The wind signifies the limitless and unassailable power of complete sincerity and truth. The two broken yin lines in the centre of the hexagram associate perfect truth with emptiness, absence—perhaps of ego, materialism, illusion etc. The Sun trigram also represents wood and here suggest a boat of special emptiness which will allow the undertaking of a special and important task i.e. 'crossing the great stream.'

Image

Wind above the waters of a marsh. The wise man deliberates about cases of litigation and delays the infliction of death.

You need to recognize and respect the innermost nature of others if you want to truly understand them and gain their respect in return.

Line readings

Line 1: *One rests in oneself. There will be good fortune. If one looks to another, one would not find rest.*

You are being dishonest and insincere with others in order to exploit them for selfish reasons.

Line 2: *One is like the crane crying out in her hidden place and her young ones responding to her. It is as if it were said, 'I have a cup of good spirits,' and the response were, 'I will partake of it with you.'*

You will experience the need to respond to the promptings of inner truth, either from your own inner nature or that of another.

Line 3: *One has met with one's mate. Now one beats one's drum, now one leaves off. Now one weeps, and now one sings.*

You have lost your integrity and self-respect by identifying too closely with another person.

Line 4: *One is like the moon nearly full, and like a horse in a chariot whose fellow disappears. There will be no error.*

You must seek solace and strength within as someone close withdraws from you.

Line 5: *One is perfectly sincere and links others to one in closest union. There will be no error.*

Your sincerity and honesty is the core around which your group coheres. You must decide if you want the group to continue. It is not your responsibility if the group fails after you withdraw.

Line 6: *One is like the crowing cock trying to mount to heaven. Even with firm correctness there will be misfortune.*

Don't seek to make what you say more impressive than its truth sufficiently makes it. Take care over how you express your self and avoid exaggerating.

Hexagram 62
Hsiao Kua—Exceeding in smallness

Component Trigrams

Primary: Chen—Thunder (upper), Ken—The Mountain (lower).
Nuclear: Tui—Marshes (above), Sun—Wind (below).

Keywords

Thunder, the mountain, appropriateness, humility, discretion.

Commentary

This is a time for you to modestly rein in your ambitions and efforts, and put them on hold. Only when appropriate circumstances present themselves should you look to humbly progress a little way along the path to your goals. You are not abandoning the correct and true path, though. You will remain committed to the perfection of honesty and sincerity, but you will proceed by more humble directions towards that worthy goal. Persist in this new path of small achievements in the correct spirit of humility and virtue and you will gain noteworthy success. These small changes that you modestly embark on will accrue disproportionately great rewards.

Judgement

There will be progress and attainment. But it will be advantageous to be firm and correct. Efforts in small affairs are advised. Efforts in large affairs are not advised. The notes of the bird on the wing descend, and it is better to descend than to rise up. There will in this way be great good fortune.

  If you strive for more modest aims and show persistence and virtue in your efforts, then you will receive significant rewards.

Interpretation

There is thunder above the mountain. The sound echoes with great power and volume, but this fades as the thunder recedes. The hexagram is concerned with modest ambition, astute self-restraint and the sensible knack of knowing when not to go for big changes. The shape of the hexagram suggests a bird. Its wings are the pairs of yin lines at the top and bottom. The action of the bird demonstrates the wisdom of humility. It is sensible to descend to a handy branch rather than continue to soar into the attractive but inhospitable wild blue yonder.

Image

Thunder beyond the hill. The wise man in his conduct exceeds in humility, in mourning exceeds in sorrow, and in his expenditure exceeds in economy.

  Be humble and modest in your conduct and your ambitions.

Attend to self-knowledge and integrity. Be sensitive and responsive to the changing times.

Line readings

Line 1: A bird flies and ascends till the issue is misfortune.

You have jumped the gun and acted before the time was right and you were properly prepared. You cannot carry out what you intended to do and you are now in a vulnerable and dangerous position. You will have to be very careful.

Line 2: *One passes by one's grandfather and meets with one's grandmother; not attempting anything against one's ruler, but meeting him as his minister. There will be no error.*

Don't be overambitious. Be satisfied with what you have already achieved.

Line 3: *One takes no extraordinary precautions against danger; and some in consequence find opportunity to assail and injure one. There will be misfortune.*

If you don't show caution then you foolishly put yourself at risk. Given the opportunity, others will take advantage of your naivety.

Line 4: *One falls into no error but meets the exigencies of the situation, without exceeding one's natural course. If one goes forward, there will be peril, and one must be cautious. There is no occasion to be using firmness perpetually.*

This is not a good time for you to take the lead in anything. You will provoke conflict with another. Withdraw from action and modestly and discreetly retire into the background. Remain true to yourself.

Line 5: *Dense clouds, but no rain, coming from the borders in the west. The prince shoots his arrow, and takes the bird in a cave.*

This is not the time for great advancement in your fortunes. Don't expect it or try for it, because you will suffer disappointment if you do.

Line 6: *One does not meet the exigency of the situation, and exceeds one's proper course. A bird flying far aloft. There will be misfortune. Calamity and self-produced injury.*

You are following an unwise and unrealistic path of ambition that will only lead you to failure. You should swallow your pride and come back down to earth. But the choice is yours.

Hexagram 63
Chi Chi—Having crossed the stream

Component Trigrams

Primary: K'an—Water (upper), Li—Fire (lower). Nuclear: Li—Fire (above), K'an—Water (below).

Keywords

Fire, water, balance, imbalance, caution, prudence, consolidation.

Commentary

You have worked hard in difficult circumstances to achieve your aim of balance and harmony, and at this point you may feel that you can withdraw, as the situation is all but resolved and success achieved. But to do this would be an error. It would disturb the balance and order you have already achieved. And though the major work has been done, something still remains to be done.

There are small tasks required to ensure that the gains already made are not lost. In a modest and calm manner you must go on, remaining committed to the true and proper way of doing things, and finish the job you started. You must do this while remembering, with due and humble acceptance of fate, that nothing ever lasts and everything is subject to change. With astute and refining adjustments your efforts should be consummated with final and rewarding success. Afterwards, however, you must expect an inevitable decline from the heights of success.

Judgement

Progress and success in small matters. There will be advantage in being firm and correct. There has been good fortune in the beginning; there may be disorder in the end.

Keep in mind that a situation that has been brought to order and harmony can quickly become unbalanced and disorganized again.

You must persevere and pay attention to small details. Remain cautious and prepared.

Interpretation

The hexagram suggests water hanging above fire. Release the water and it douses the fire. Heighten the flames and the water evaporates. But neither happens as the elements of the situation are in balance, neither invading the other's position. This suggestion of order and balance is added to by the regularly alternating yin and yang lines. Also in relation to the idea of symmetrical balance: the upper primary trigram represents danger, but the lower represents intelligent foresight. (Note also the symmetrical inversion of the nuclear trigrams). The name of the hexagram refers to a situation of completeness and success at the end of a long and testing undertaking. However, there are still some things to be done to finally secure the success.

Image

Water above fire. The wise man thinks of evil that may come, and beforehand guards against it.

At a time of balance and order the wise man begins preparing for the bad times that will follow.

Line readings

Line 1: *A driver drags back his wheel; a fox has wet his tail. There will be no error.*

Don't get just get swept along with the changes and developments that are taking place. You must go at your own pace and follow only the dictates of your conscience and your judgement.

Line 2: *A wife has lost her carriage-screen. There is no occasion to go in pursuit of it. In seven days she will find it.*

A recognition or a union that you seek is not being granted. You must accept this. Cultivate your inner self and bide your time. The situation will change.

Line 3: *One attacked the Demon region, but was three years in subduing it. Small men should not be employed in such enterprises.*

When you are in the process of developing your knowledge, your curiosity and desire to learn may inadvertently lead you into intimidating or upsetting others. Take care over this.

Line 4: *One has rags provided against any leak in one's boat, and is on guard all day long.*

Even the most favourable of times will end, and change into times of misfortune and hardship. Remain prepared at all times for unexpected problems and setbacks.

Line 5: *The neighbour in the east slaughters an ox for his sacrifice; but this is not equal to the small spring sacrifice of the neighbour in the west, whose sincerity receives the blessing.*

Don't try to fool people or show them disrespect. Be honest and sincere. Remain true to yourself.

Line 6: *One has even one's head immersed. The situation is perilous.*

Having completed an undertaking and effected a change, whether for the good or the worse, you must continue to move on. You cannot stay where you are. Neither can you return to the way things were. Things done, are as they always will be. Leave them behind and keep going forward.

Hexagram 64
Wei Chi—Having not yet crossed the stream

Component Trigrams

Primary: Li—Fire (upper), K'an—Water (lower). Nuclear: K'an—Water (above), Li—Fire (below).

Keywords

Fire, water, disharmony, incoherence, lack of order, caution, prudence.

Commentary

The time of harmony and balance has passed and disorder has taken its place. This is the new situation you find yourself in. Big challenges lie ahead as you strive to restore coherence. But disorder and disharmony are natural aspects of human life and the ability to respond appropriately to such situations is a great advantage. Examine closely the basis of the present situation and make sensible and realistic assessments about what it is possible to achieve. You must tackle the problems with careful thought and planning. Don't try to be clever in any way, or to take short-cuts. You should spend time and effort in developing harmonious relations with others. Your action to turn the situation around should be characterized by honest and humble persistence and a determination never to deviate from your principled motives and conduct. In this way you will be promoting the emergence of new order and harmony.

Judgement

Progress and success. Yet for a young fox that has nearly crossed the stream, but has immersed his tail in the water, there will be no advantage in any way.

Immature bravado, naivety and inexperience will find only trouble and problems when it tries to act or make real progress. Caution and preparedness are required, particularly at the moment of success.

Interpretation

In the hexagram, fire is above water. Fire burns upwards. Water flows downwards. And never the twain shall meet. The two forces are not in harmony and neither can affect the other. The hexagram suggests forces which are polar opposites but are not arranged so that they are complementary to each other. The arduous effort to create order out of such disorder will also require great caution and firm discipline. The hexagram's name refers to the tremendous undertaking not yet completed.

Image

Fire above water. The wise man carefully discriminates among the qualities of things, and the different positions they naturally occupy.

Striving to ensure that things are in their proper places and in their proper relations to one another is how order is created. When things are in balance and harmony then all is well.

Line readings

Line 1: *One is like a fox whose tail gets immersed. There will be occasion for regret.*

It is not yet time to act. Be more patient and less impulsive.

Line 2: *One drags back one's carriage-wheel. With firmness and correctness there will be good fortune.*

Keep waiting patiently, but prepare for action by planning well.

Line 3: *With the state of things not yet remedied, one advances on; which will lead to evil. But there will be advantage in trying to cross the great stream.*

Don't leap into action. It may be better to enlist the help of others in taking a new direction rather than attempting to forge ahead on your own.

Line 4: *By firm correctness one obtains good fortune, so that all occasion for repentance disappears. Let one stir oneself up, as if one were invading the Demon region, where for three years rewards will come to one and one's troops from the great kingdom.*

You must act now, and expect to encounter trying difficulties as you go forward. You must not deviate from your course as you engage with problems. Your struggle is wresting order from disorder.

Line 5: *By firm correctness one obtains good fortune, and has no occasion for repentance. One has the brightness of a wise man, and the possession of sincerity. There will be good fortune.*

You have accomplished what you set out to do and things are falling into their final places. You are in the midst of a new beginning and you feel satisfied and full of clarity. Others around you are aware of this.

Line 6: *One is full of confidence and therefore feasting quietly. There will be no error. If one cherish this confidence till one is like the fox who gets his head immersed, one will fail of what is right.*

You can celebrate final success with others. But don't forsake your principles or lose your integrity by indulging in excess.

Sovereign Hexagrams

The ancient Chinese believed that twelve of the hexagrams related to months in their lunar calendar, and that if they were drawn in a consultation they provided a guide as to the likely date of any event indicated in the hexagram. These twelve hexagrams were called the Sovereign hexagrams and they are: T'ai, Ta Chuang, Kuai, Ch'ien, Kou, Tun, P'i, Kuan, Po, K'un, Fu, and Lin. The table below lists the Sovereign hexagrams, with the names and the time spans of the fortnight periods they are taken to indicate.

Hexagram	**Fortnight name**	**Beginning**
T'ai		
	Beginning of Spring	5th of February
	The Rains	20th of February
Ta Chuang		
	Awakening of Creatures	7th of March
	Spring Equinox	22nd of March
Kuai		
	Clear and Bright	6th of April
	Grain Rain	21st of April
Ch'ien		
	Beginning of Summer	6th of May
	Lesser Fulness	22nd of May
Kou		
	Grain in Ear	7th of June
	Summer Solstice	22nd of June
Tun		
	Lesser Heat	8th of July
	Greater Heat	24th of July
P'i		
	Beginning of Autumn	8th of August
	End of Heat	24th of August
Kuan		
	White Dews	8th of September
	Autumn Equinox	24th of September

Hexagram	**Fortnight name**	**Beginning**
Po		
	Cold Dews	9th of October
	Descent of Hoar Frost	24th of October
K'un		
	Beginning of Winter	8th of November
	Lesser Snow	23rd of November
Fu		
	Greater Snow	7th of December
	Winter Solstice	22nd of December
Lin		
	Lesser Cold	6th of January
	Greater Cold	21st of January

Glossary

coin method here refers to the three coins that are thrown as part of the procedure of consulting the I Ching.

Confucius westerners use Confucius (551-479 BC) as the spelling for K'ung Fu-tzu—Master K'ung—China's first and most famous philosopher. Confucius devoted himself to learning and to teaching others. Confucius himself never wrote down his own philosophy. The book known as the 'Analects', which records all the "Confucius said, . . ." aphorisms, was compiled by his students after his death.

Confucianism the philosophical system founded on the teaching of Confucius. It dominated Chinese social and political life for most of Chinese history and largely influenced the cultures of Korea, Japan, and Indochina. Confucianism supported political authority using the theory of the mandate of heaven. It sought to help the rulers maintain domestic order, preserve tradition, and maintain a constant standard of living for the taxpaying peasants. It trained its adherents in benevolence, traditional rituals, filial piety, loyalty, respect for superiors and for the aged, and principled flexibility in advising rulers. Confucianism absorbed the metaphysical doctrines of yin (the female principle) and yang (the male principle) from the I Ching.

consulter a person who consults the I Ching.

divination the art of discerning future events.

Fu Hsi the legendary creator of the trigrams and thus the originator of the I Ching.

hexagram a six-line figure, composed of a combination of broken (yin) lines and unbroken (yang) lines.

hexagram key a table giving the numbers of the sixty-four hexagrams created by the combinations of the eight primary trigrams.

hexagram system the sixty-four hexagrams of the I Ching collected together with their accompanying texts.

Lao-Tse the ancient Chinese philosopher Lao-Tse (551-479 BC). He wrote the Tao Te Ching, the philosophical basis of Taoism.

moving lines lines in a hexagram which have line-values of 6 or

9 and which will imminently change into their opposite principle, be it yin or yang.

New Age a late-twentieth century movement or philosophy embracing holistic, ecological and spiritual approaches to living.

nuclear trigram the second, third and fourth lines (below), and the third, fourth and fifth lines in a hexagram (above).

oracle a source of prophecies or predictions about future events.

primary trigram the bottom three and top three lines in a hexagram.

synchronicity the theory that Jung derived from his reading and acquaintance with the I Ching. Synchronicity states that everything that occurs at the same moment in time is linked and mutually influencing because of its quality of simultaneity.

T'ai Chi the 'ridgepole' of Taoist philosophy which is the fixed point of the universe and the origin of yin and yang.

Tao the Way or One True Path of the universe, as expressed by the philosopher Lao-Tse.

Taoism the term refers to the philosophy outlined in the Tao Te Ching (The Way and Its Power), by the philosopher Lao-Tse; and also to China's ancient Taoist religion. Next to Confucianism it is the second major belief system in traditional Chinese thought. The harmony of opposites (T'ai Chi) is achieved through a blend of the yin (feminine force) and the yang (masculine force); this harmony can be cultivated through creative quietude (wu wei), an effortless action whose power (de or te) maintains equanimity and balance. Taoism teaches the devotee to lead a long and tranquil life through the elimination of one's desires and aggressive impulses. Hence the wise person accepts life's changes.

trigram a three-line figure, composed of a combination of broken (yin) lines and unbroken (yang) lines.

yang the primal, masculine principle of the universe, in complementary polar opposition to the yin principle.

yang line A single unbroken line in a trigram or hexagram.

yarrow sticks short sticks, traditionally from the yarrow plant but now referring to any type of wood, which are used as part of the method for consulting the I Ching.

yin the primal, feminine principle of the universe, in complementary polar opposition to the yang principle.

yin line a single broken line in a trigram or a hexagram.